W9-AGE-892

SAY IT WITH CHARTS

THE EXECUTIVE'S GUIDE
TO SUCCESSFUL PRESENTATIONS

SAY IT WITH CHARTS

THE EXECUTIVE'S GUIDE
TO SUCCESSFUL PRESENTATIONS

GENE ZELAZNY

DOW JONES-IRWIN
Homewood, Illinois 60430

GRAPHIC CONSULTANT:
VERA DEUTSCH

EDITOR:
SARA ROCHE

© DOW JONES-IRWIN, 1985

All rights reserved. No part of this publication may be
reproduced, stored in a retrieval system, or transmitted,
in any form or by any means, electronic, mechanical,
photocopying, recording, or otherwise, without the prior
written permission of the publisher.

This publication is designed to provide accurate and
authoritative information in regard to the subject matter
covered. It is sold with the understanding that the
publisher is not engaged in rendering legal, accounting, or
other professional service. If legal advice or other expert
assistance is required, the services of a competent
professional person should be sought.

*From a Declaration of Principles jointly adopted by a Committee
of the American Bar Association and a Committee of Publishers.*

ISBN 0-87094-533-5

Library of Congress Catalog Card No. 83-73367

Printed in the United States of America

3 4 5 6 7 8 9 0 MP 2 1 0 9 8 7 6 5

To Ken Haemer

If we define originality as "undiscovered plagiarism," then this book is original. Much of the credit for the ideas presented in this book belongs to the late Kenneth W. Haemer (formerly Manager, Presentation Research, AT&T). Over the years Ken was both mentor and friend. Thank you, Ken. I miss you.

If Ken made me think, then McKinsey & Company, Inc., provided me with a home to apply and advance my ideas. And so, let me also thank the hundreds of professional consultants I work with at McKinsey. It's a privilege and a pleasure.

Last, many, many thanks to all of you who have assisted in making this book a reality.

CONTENTS

Section 2

USING CHARTS 73

"What do you mean, what does it mean?"

INTRODUCTION

It's 9:00 a.m. on the third Tuesday of the month, time for the monthly meeting of the Steering Committee. To set the rest of the day's proceedings in perspective, the committee chairman has asked a bright, fast-rising manager—let's call him Frank—to prepare a brief presentation on the state of the industry in which we compete and our company's performance as a stepping stone for new investment opportunities.

Intent on doing a good job, Frank has done much research, worked on his story line, and prepared a series of visual aids to help him say it with charts. Like most of us, Frank realizes that charts are an important form of language. They're important because, when well conceived and designed, they help us communicate more quickly and more clearly than we would if we left the data in tabular form.

When charts *aren't* well conceived or designed, as we're about to see in Frank's examples, they serve more to confuse than to clarify. Let's sit with the audience and listen to Frank's presentation as we comment, quietly, on the effectiveness of his visuals.

Frank begins: Good morning ladies and gentlemen. My purpose is to present a brief overview of our industry and our company's performance. My objective is to gain your support for expanding into developing countries. I've designed a few visual aids to better place my findings in perspective.

First, let me point out that we compete in a healthy industry. As you can clearly see from this exhibit, for the 11 measures of performance shown across the top and the three types of companies within the industry listed down the side, performance is excellent.

And there you sit in the audience, wondering whether your eyesight is failing, as you try in vain to read the numbers.

▶ 1

SUMMARY OF THE MARGINAL CONTRIBUTION
INCREASES PROJECTED FOR THE MARKETING IMPROVEMENT PROGRAMS
BY BRANCH AND REGION

Frank continues: Within the industry, our performance has been outstanding. For instance, our sales have grown considerably since 1979, in spite of the decline in 1981 which, as you know, was the result of the strike.

"Oops," you whisper, "did I just miss something? I could swear I heard Frank say that sales have grown considerably, but what I see is a series of pie charts that show our major product's share increasing. Oh! Wait a minute. I see! He's referring to the figures underneath each pie. . . ."

▶ 2

OUR COMPANY'S SALES TREND, 1979-1984
$ millions   ■ Major product's share

1979	1980	1981
$1.2	$1.8	$0.9

1982	1983	1984
$2.0	$2.9	$3.4

Frank goes on: Compared with our four major competitors, we rank first in return on investment with 14 percent. . . .

"What ranks first? Who ranks first?" you say. "From the visual, I thought the point was that ROI has been fluctuating."

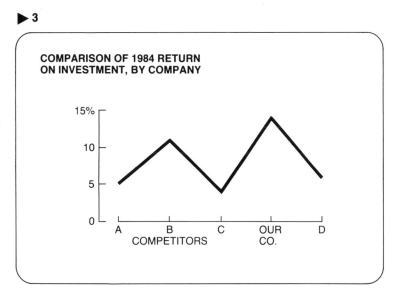

▶ 3

COMPARISON OF 1984 RETURN ON INVESTMENT, BY COMPANY

. . . and our market share has increased since 1979 along with that of one competitor, while the other three lost share.

You sigh in frustration "Has someone spiked my orange juice? Why do I feel that my eyes and ears aren't talking to one another, that I'm receiving mixed signals? Is it perhaps that the visuals I see are not supporting the messages I hear?"

▶ 4

MARKET SHARE TRENDS, BY COMPANY 1979-1984

Frank proceeds: Given these sales, ROI, and market-share trends, we recommend expanding the selling effort for our major product into developing countries. We believe these markets hold considerable potential. Since you may not understand this visual, let me explain it. What I've done is shown the total size of the market worldwide in 1984 and projected it to 1990. On the basis of a lot of research, we forecast that the market will increase from $8 billion to over $11 billion. Then I divided the totals by the 11 countries that make up the market and showed the size of each. Then I calculated the average annual compound

▶ 5

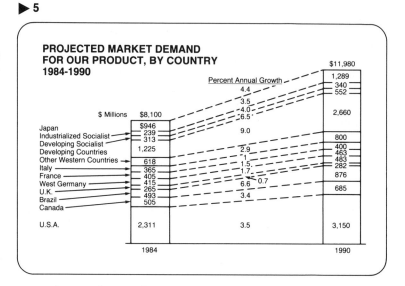

growth rate for each country and listed it in the center. As you can see from these figures, the developing countries are projected to show the fastest growth.

Now I feel your nudge and hear your aside: "Isn't it remarkable how these visual aids designed to aid speakers require so much speaker aid to be understood. I always thought that a picture was worth 1,000 words, not that it required them."

4

Frank: If we are to move ahead, however, we need first to persuade top management that the political and social climate in these developing countries will not interfere with our plans. A recent poll of 16 top management members reveals they are almost evenly split for and against investing in these countries.

By now, your social unrest is hard to contain, and the pie chart conjures visions of dessert at lunch.

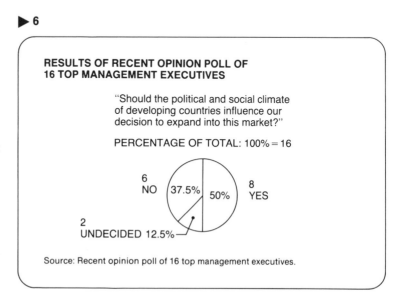

▶ 6

RESULTS OF RECENT OPINION POLL OF 16 TOP MANAGEMENT EXECUTIVES

"Should the political and social climate of developing countries influence our decision to expand into this market?"

PERCENTAGE OF TOTAL: 100% = 16

6 NO   37.5%   50%   8 YES

2 UNDECIDED 12.5%

Source: Recent opinion poll of 16 top management executives.

Frank's intention was right: he meant to use charts to support his presentation. His execution was not good: he developed a series of charts that were illegible or unintelligible and that detracted from his presentation. Let's review his charts and see why they don't work.

Visual number ▶ 1 is illegible. Like all illegible visuals, it suffers from the APK—anxious parade of knowledge—syndrome. This is usually the case when the presenter is more concerned with what's been put *into* the chart than in what the audience gets *out* of it.

What Frank didn't realize is that a chart used in a visual presentation must be at least twice as simple and four times as bold as one used in a report. It's the same as the distinction between a billboard that must be read and understood in the time you drive past it and a magazine advertisement that you can study in detail.

At the other extreme is the last chart, number ▶ **6,** which is so simple that it is not needed; the message could have been expressed with words alone. In addition to overly simple charts, there are other situations when you're better off without a chart:

1.   Sometimes the chart denotes a sense of accuracy that may be misleading, as is the case with projections or ranges that may be tenuous.

2.   Sometimes there are sets of data that the audience or reader has become comfortable with, such as the company's profit and loss statement, and changing the form to a chart could be confusing.

3.   Certain individuals may be unaccustomed to, or resistant to, or skeptical about the use of charts.

With charts, a good rule is "fewer is better." Producing charts is time-consuming and expensive. Also, the more charts we use, the less people remember. Use one chart in a report or presentation, and it will receive 100 percent of the audience's attention; use 100, and none will be memorable.

Chart 5, the one describing the world market, is what I call a "charttable"; it can't make up its mind whether to be a chart or a table and decides to be both. The hope is that if the chart doesn't work, the information may. In most cases, neither does. Undoubtedly, this chart helped Frank figure out the important relationships—in this case, the comparison of projected growth rates by country. However, Frank did not translate the data from the form that helped him analyze the problem to a simpler chart that emphasized the results of his analyses.

The remaining three charts, ▶ **2, 3,** and **4,** suffer from what is probably the major problem facing most of us when we translate data into chart form: the wrong form for the message. In Chart 2, pie charts were chosen where a line chart is called for; in Chart 3, a line chart was used where a bar chart would be better; in 4, we see a dot chart instead of column charts.

Here is what these three charts should have looked like to support the spoken message more quickly and clearly.

Sales have increased from $1.2 million in 1979 to $3.4 million in 1984 despite the decline in 1981 caused by the strike.

▶ 2

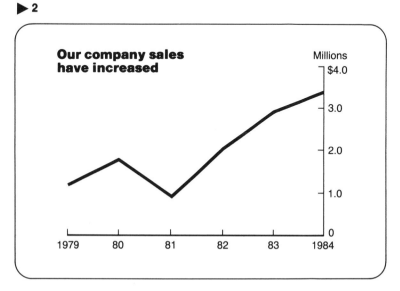

Compared with our four major competitors, we rank first with a 14 percent return on investment in 1984.

▶ 3

Our market share has increased 4 percentage points from 11 percent in 1979 to 15 percent today. Of our four competitors, B also improved, while C, A, and D lost share.

▶ 4

Our company's market share has improved since 1979

Now these charts work. In each case, the chart form supports the message expressed in the title, and the title reinforces the point the chart demonstrates. In all cases, the message comes across faster and better than it would if the data were left in table form.

And there you have the purpose of this book. Its goal is **to help you say it with charts by choosing and using charts that will work for you and your audience** no matter where the charts are used—be it in business presentations or reports, in your management information system, in computer graphics software packages, in annual reports, or in magazines or newspaper articles.

In Section 1, we'll work our way through the process that moves us from data to chart. **In Section 2,** we'll examine a portfolio of finished charts that you can refer to for ideas the next time the need comes up.

As I said before, charts *are* an important form of language. But as is true of any language we want to become proficient in, it takes time and patience to learn the vocabulary, and practice until the skill becomes second nature. Since no one learns by reading, only by doing, I've incorporated work projects so you can practice as you read. So take pencil in hand, and let's move on to the process of choosing charts.

Section 1

CHOOSING CHARTS

No matter how many business graphics we see in various kinds of communications—including tables, organization charts, flow diagrams, matrixes, maps—when it comes to quantitative charts, there are only five basic chart forms to choose from. As shown here in simple terms, these are:

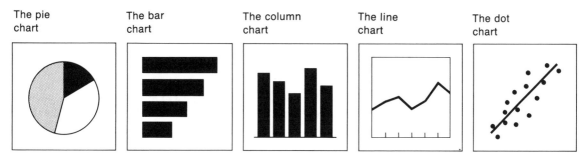

| The pie chart | The bar chart | The column chart | The line chart | The dot chart |

Now we know where we're going; the question is, how do we get there? With the following diagram, let me summarize the process that moves us from the data we start with to the specific chart we end with.

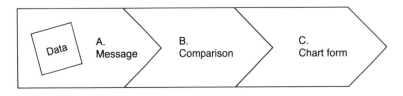

Step A:

DETERMINE YOUR MESSAGE
(from data to message).

The key to choosing the appropriate chart form is for *you*, as the designer, to be clear, first and foremost, about the specific point you want to make.

Step B:

IDENTIFY THE COMPARISON
(from message to comparison).

The message you've determined will always imply one of five basic kinds of comparison: component, item, time series, frequency distribution, or correlation.

Step C:

SELECT THE CHART FORM
(from comparison to chart).

Each comparison will lead, in turn, to one of the five chart forms.

Let's discuss each step in detail.

A. DETERMINE <u>YOUR</u> MESSAGE

(from data to message)

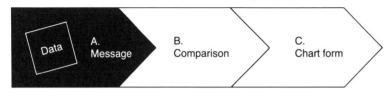

Choosing a chart form without a message in mind is like trying to color coordinate your wardrobe while blindfolded.

Choosing the correct chart form depends completely on *your* being clear about what *your* message is. It is not the data—be they dollars, percentages, liters, yen, etc.— that determine the chart. It is not the measure—be it profits, return on investment, compensation, etc.—that determines the chart. Rather, it is *your* message, what *you* want to show, the specific point *you* want to make.

To stress the importance of this first step, sketch as many charts as you can think of in the empty boxes on the next two pages using the data (percentage of sales by region for each company) shown in the upper right-hand box. Don't worry about accuracy—your goal is to draw as many charts as you can before turning to page 14.

PROJECT

Sketch as many charts as you can think of using these data: the more the better.

Percentage of January Sales by Region

	Co. A	Co. B
North	13%	39%
South	35	6
East	27	27
West	25	28

WHICH CHART WOULD YOU CHOOSE?

▶1

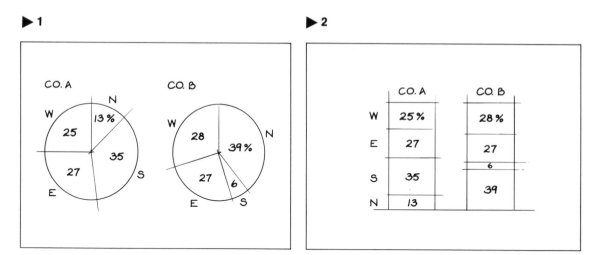

CO. A
N 13%
W 25
35
27 S
E

CO. B
W 28
39%
N
27 6
E S

▶2

CO. A
W	25%
E	27
S	35
N	13

CO. B
| 28% |
| 27 |
| 6 |
| 39 |

▶3

CO. A
N 13%
S 35
E 27
W 25

CO. B
39%
6
27
28

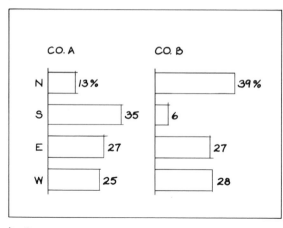

▶4

CO. A
S 35%
E 27
W 25
N 13

CO. B
N 39%
W 28
E 27
S 6

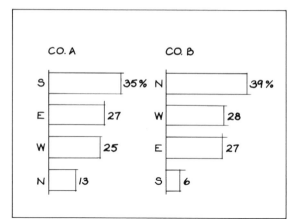

▶5

CO. A   CO. B
35%   S   6%
27   E   27
25   W   28
13   N   39

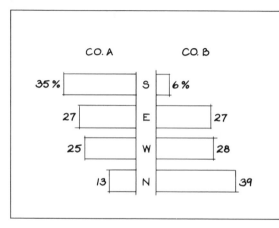

▶6

S CO. A   35%
   CO. B 6%
E CO. A   27
   CO. B   27
W CO. A   25
   CO. B   28
N CO. A   13
   CO. B   39

14

The charts shown on the facing page may be among those you sketched. All the better if you thought of others. But a question remains.

WHICH CHART WOULD YOU CHOOSE?

It all depends! It all depends on the specific point *you* want to make—*your* message. Each chart shown, simply as a function of the way it's organized, is best equipped to emphasize a particular message.

For instance, showing the data as a couple of pie charts or 100 percent columns, you would be emphasizing that:

▶ **1** ▶ **2** The mix of sales is different for Companies A and B.

Or you may have shown the data as two sets of bar charts, sequencing the bars in the order the data were presented in the table. Now the chart is stressing the message that:

▶ **3** The percentage of sales for both Companies A and B varies by region.

On the other hand, you could have ranked the percentage of sales for each company in descending (or ascending) order, now stressing the point that:

▶ **4** Company A is highest in the South; Company B is highest in the North. Or, Company A is lowest in the North; Company B is lowest in the South.

By structuring the bars in a mirror image around the regions, we now demonstrate that:

▶ **5** Company A's share of sales is highest in the South where Company B's is the weakest.

By grouping the bars against a common base, we now compare the gaps by region, showing that:

▶ **6** In the South, Company A leads B by a wide margin; in the East and West, the two are competitive; in the North, A lags B.

Now, it's possible—even probable—that in the early stages of deciding what your message should be, you may need to sketch a number of charts that look at the data from various points of view. A more efficient approach is to highlight the aspect of the data that seems most important and settle on the message that brings out that aspect.

For example, looking at this simplified table, there are three possible aspects of the data that could be highlighted and turned into messages.

Your attention might focus on the overall sales trend from January through May; how the dollar value of sales has changed over time. In that case, your message would be that "Sales have risen steadily since January."

Sales by Product, $000

	Product A	B	C	Total
Jan.	88	26	7	121
Feb.	94	30	8	132
Mar.	103	36	8	147
Apr.	113	39	7	159
May	122	40	13	175

On the other hand, you might want to focus on a single point in time. Reading the figures across for May, for example, you might take note of the ranking of sales for Products A, B, and C. In that case, your message could be: "In May, sales of Product A exceeded those of B and C by a wide margin."

Sales by Product, $000

	Product A	B	C	Total
Jan.	88	26	7	121
Feb.	94	30	8	132
Mar.	103	36	8	147
Apr.	113	39	7	159
May	122	40	13	175

Looking at the same May data from yet another perspective, you might focus on the percentage of total sales accounted for by each product. Then your message might be: "In May, Product A accounted for the largest share of total company sales."

Sales by Product, $000

	Product A	B	C	Total
Jan.	88	26	7	121
Feb.	94	30	8	132
Mar.	103	36	8	147
Apr.	113	39	7	159
May	122	40	13	175
	70%	23%	7%	100%

Note that for these last two examples, we used nearly the same aspect of the data to come up with different messages. The decision to emphasize ranking or share is up to you, and that decision will give you your message.

Suppose you have other data from the same company.

This table shows the distribution of sales by size of sale at one point in time, May. Here your message might be: "In May, most sales were in the $1,000 to $2,000 range."

Number of Sales by Size of Sale, May

Size of sale	Number of sales
<$1,000	15
1,000-1,999	30
2,000-2,999	12
3,000-3,999	8
4,000 +	5

This last set of data shows the relationship of the salesperson's experience to the sales he or she generates. Noting that salesperson P, with only two years' experience, generates $23,000 in sales, while salesperson Q, with more than twice the experience, generates only one-quarter the volume would indicate the message that: "There is no relationship between sales and experience."

Relationship of Salesperson's Experience to Sales

Salesperson	Years of experience	Amount of sales
P	2	$23,000
Q	5	6,000
R	7	17,000
S	15	9,000
T	22	12,000

As we've seen, this first step, determining your message, must be completed before you can select the appropriate chart form. Having spent all that time and energy doing so, you may as well make the most of the effort and *let the message become the title of the chart*. Let me elaborate.

For many of the charts we see, the title is little more than a cryptic heading, such as:

COMPANY SALES TREND

PRODUCTIVITY BY REGION

PERCENTAGE OF ASSETS BY DIVISION

DISTRIBUTION OF EMPLOYEES BY AGE

RELATIONSHIP OF COMPENSATION TO PROFITABILITY

These titles describe the subject of the chart, but they don't say what's important about it. What about sales performance? What about the distribution of employees? What about the relationship between compensation and profitability? Don't keep it a secret; let your message head the chart. In so doing, you reduce the risk that the reader will misunderstand, and you make sure he or she **focuses on the aspect of the data you want to emphasize.**

Let's look at a couple of examples that demonstrate the difference and establish the advantage of message titles over the topic titles just shown.

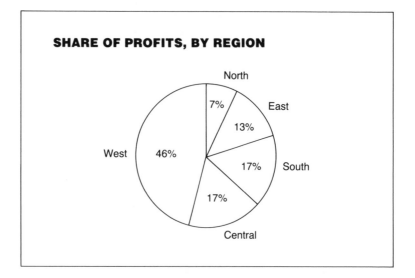

SHARE OF PROFITS, BY REGION

Here, the title states the topic of the chart, leaving you to determine the significance of what the chart shows. Studying the chart, most readers would probably focus on the West, believing the message to be emphasized is that the **"West accounts for almost half of profits."**

However, that may not be the point that the designer wants you to focus on. He or she may wish to stress that the *"North* generates the smallest share of profits." In short, with the topic title, you run the risk of being misunderstood. Substituting the message title, **"North generates the smallest share of profits"** reduces that risk by focusing the reader's attention on the aspect of the data we want to stress.

In this second example, the title merely identifies what the trend line stands for—NUMBER OF CONTRACTS—and serves to distinguish the topic of this line chart from that of other line charts we might see in a report or presentation. However, studying the trend, here are four possible aspects we may want to stress.

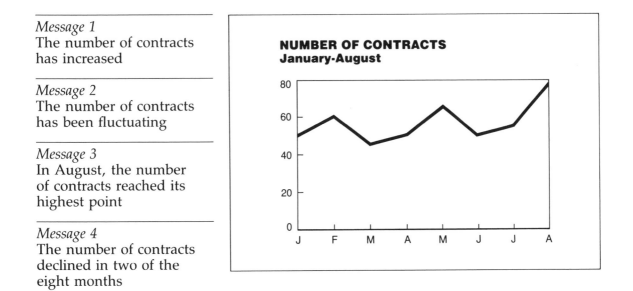

Message 1
The number of contracts has increased

Message 2
The number of contracts has been fluctuating

Message 3
In August, the number of contracts reached its highest point

Message 4
The number of contracts declined in two of the eight months

NUMBER OF CONTRACTS
January-August

To assist readers, let's select **the one message** we wish to emphasize to head the chart.

A message title is similar to a headline in your newspaper or magazine; it is brief and to the point and summarizes what you're about to read. For the cryptic headings we showed before, here's what the message titles might look like:

Topic title: COMPANY SALES TREND
Message title: **Company sales have doubled**

Topic title: PRODUCTIVITY BY REGION
Message title: **Region C ranks fourth in productivity**

Topic title: PERCENTAGE OF ASSETS BY DIVISION
Message title: **Division B accounts for 30% of the assets**

Topic title: DISTRIBUTION OF EMPLOYEES BY AGE
Message title: **Most employees are between 35 and 45 years old**

Topic title: RELATIONSHIP OF COMPENSATION TO PROFITABILITY
Message title: **There is no relationship between compensation and profitability**

Once you've determined *your* message, you'll find the process becomes very specific. So let's move on to the second step, identifying the kind of comparison implied in your message.

B. IDENTIFY THE COMPARISON

(from message to comparison)

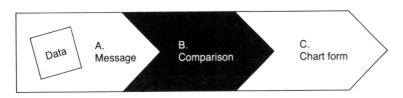

If Step 1 is the message we start with and Step 3 is the chart we end with, this step is the link between the two.

What's important to recognize here is that any message—that is, any point from the data you wish to emphasize—will always lead to one of five basic kinds of comparison, which I've chosen to call *component, item, time series, frequency distribution,* and *correlation.*

Let's see examples of messages that imply each one of these comparisons. At the same time, let me define the comparisons and give you clues—trigger words—for recognizing them in messages you derive from the data.

1. COMPONENT COMPARISON

In a component comparison, we are interested primarily in showing the *size* of each part *as a percentage* of the total. For example:

¶ In May, Product A *accounted* for the largest *share of total* company sales.
¶ Client *share of market* in 1984 is less than 10 percent of the industry.
¶ Two sources contributed almost *half of total* corporate funds.

Any time your message contains words such as *share, percentage of total, accounted for* X *percent,* you can be sure you're dealing with a component comparison.

2. ITEM COMPARISON

In an item comparison, we want to compare how things *rank:* are they about *the same,* or is one *more* or *less* than the others? For example:

¶ In May, sales of *Product A exceeded* those of *Products B and C.*

¶ Client's return on sales *ranks* fourth.

¶ Turnover rates in the six departments are *about equal.*

Words indicating *larger than, smaller than,* or *equal* are clues to an item comparison.

3. TIME SERIES COMPARISON

This comparison is the one we're most familiar with. We're not interested in the size of each part in a total or how they're ranked, but in how they *change over time,* whether the trend over weeks, months, quarters, years is *increasing, decreasing,* or *remaining constant.* For example:

¶ Sales *have risen* steadily since January.

¶ Return on investment *has decreased* sharply over the past five years.

¶ Interest rates *have fluctuated* over the past seven quarters.

Clues to look for in your message are words like *change, grow, rise, decline, increase, decrease, fluctuate.*

4. FREQUENCY DISTRIBUTION COMPARISON

This kind of comparison shows *how many items fall into a series of progressive numerical ranges.* For instance, we use a frequency distribution to show how many employees earn less than, say, $10,000, how many earn between $10,000 and $20,000, etc.; or how much of the population is under 10 years old, how many people are between 10 and 20, between 20 and 30, etc. Typical messages might be:

¶ In May, *most sales* were in the *$1,000 to $2,000 range.*

¶ The *majority of shipments* are delivered in *five to six days.*

¶ The *age distribution* of company employees differs sharply from that of our competitor.

Terms to look for that suggest this kind of comparison are *x to y range, concentration,* as well as the words *frequency* and *distribution* themselves.

5. CORRELATION COMPARISON

A correlation comparison shows *whether the relationship between two variables follows—*or fails to follow—*the pattern you would normally expect.* For example, you would normally expect profits to increase as sales increase; you would normally expect sales to increase as the size of the discount offered increases.

Whenever your message includes words like *related to, increases with, decreases with, changes with, varies with,* or the converse such as *doesn't increase with,* it's an instant clue that you're showing a correlation comparison. For example:

¶ Sales performance in May shows *no relationship between* sales and the salesperson's experience.
¶ Chief executive officer compensation *does not vary* with size of company.
¶ Size of policy *increases with* policyholder income.

There you have them, the five kinds of comparison implied in any of the messages you'll be deriving from tabular data. Stated simply:

Component: Percentage of a total.

Item: Ranking of items.

Time Series: Changes over time.

Frequency Distribution: Items within ranges.

Correlation: Relationship between variables.

With this in mind and pencil in hand, study the following 12 typical messages derived from tabular data and identify the kind of comparison implied by each message. Look for the clues—the trigger words—in each, and, if necessary, look back to the definition and the examples we've just discussed. Check your answers with those shown upside down at the bottom of the page.

Typical Messages	Comparison?

1. Sales are forecast to increase over the next 10 years _____

2. The largest number of employees earns between $20,000 and $25,000 _____

3. Higher price of gasoline brands does not indicate better performance _____

4. In September, the turnover rates for the six divisions were about the same _____

5. The sales manager spends only 15% of his time in the field _____

6. Size of merit increases is not related to tenure _____

7. Last year, most turnover was in the 30 to 35 age group _____

8. Region C ranks last in productivity _____

9. Our company's earnings per share is declining _____

10. The largest share of total funds is allocated for manufacturing _____

11. There is a relationship between profitability and compensation _____

12. In August, two plants outproduced the other six by a wide margin _____

ANSWERS

4. Item	8. Item	12. Item
3. Correlation	7. Frequency Distribution	11. Correlation
2. Frequency Distribution	6. Correlation	10. Component
1. Time Series	5. Component	9. Time Series

Having moved from the data to your message and from your message to a comparison, we're now ready to proceed with the final step—from the comparison to the chart form most appropriate for your message.

C. SELECT THE CHART FORM
(from comparison to chart)

Now you have seen that, no matter what your message is, it will always imply one of the five kinds of comparison. It should come as no surprise that, no matter what the comparison is, it will always lead to one of the five basic chart forms: the pie chart, the bar chart, the column chart, the line chart, and the dot chart.

The pie chart   The bar chart   The column chart   The line chart   The dot chart

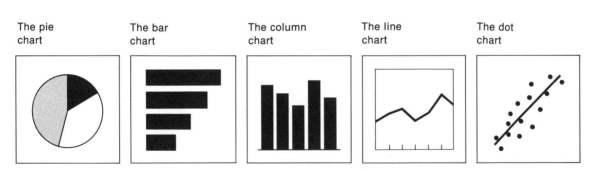

I've observed that the *pie chart* is the most popular. It shouldn't be; it's the least practical and should account for little more than 5 percent of the charts used in a presentation or report.

On the other hand, the *bar chart* is the least appreciated. It should receive much more attention; it's the most versatile and should account for as much as 25 percent of all charts used.

I consider the *column chart* to be "good old reliable" and the *line chart* to be the workhorse; these two should account for half of all charts used.

The *dot chart* is slowly gaining favor. While intimidating at first glance, it is also sophisticated and definitely has its place 10 percent of the time.

That accounts for 90 percent. The remainder is likely to be these chart forms used in combination—say, a line chart with a column chart or a pie chart with a column chart.

Let's recognize that each chart form, simply as a function of the way it's designed, is best equipped to illustrate one of the five comparisons.

This matrix illustrates the primary choices. Down the side are the five basic chart forms. Across the top are the five kinds of comparison we've just discussed. For time series, frequency distributions, and correlations, you have two choices of chart forms. Deciding which to use is a function of the amount of data you're plotting. For a time series or frequency distribution, use the column chart when you have few (say, six or seven) data points; use the line chart when you have many. For a correlation comparison, use the bar chart to show few data, the dot chart when you have many.

Let's work our way through the matrix and see why each chart form is recommended to show each comparison. In the process, we'll discuss how to make the most of the chart forms and present variations for each that provide additional information.

KINDS OF COMPARISON

COMPONENT | ITEM | TIME SERIES | FREQUENCY | CORRELATION

BASIC CHART FORMS

PIE | BAR | COLUMN | LINE | DOT

As we proceed, keep in mind that choosing, and especially using, charts is not an exact science. And so you'll note a liberal sprinkling of qualifiers, such as, generally, occasionally, most of the time, some of the time, etc., all of which imply that your judgment must play a role in deciding how best to design the charts. The options presented in the matrix, along with the suggestions for making the most of charts, are guidelines. More often than not, however, you'll find these guidelines will serve you well.

Before turning the page for a specific discussion of each comparison and its recommended chart form, I suggest that you pause for a while and skip to the second section of this book where I present a portfolio of all these charts at work. Browse through this shopping list of charts to gain an appreciation of how effective charts can be when they are well conceived and designed.

1. COMPONENT COMPARISON

A component comparison can best be demonstrated using a pie chart. Because a circle gives such a clear impression of being a total, a pie chart is ideally suited for the one—and only—purpose it serves: showing the size of each part as a percentage of some whole, such as companies that make up an industry.

THE PIE CHART

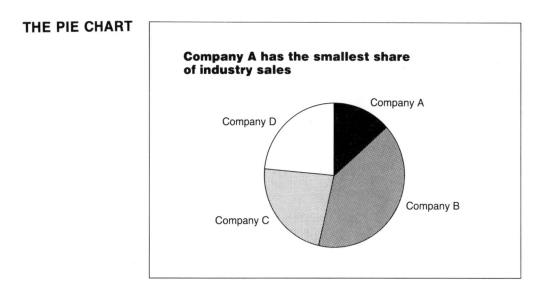

To make the most of pie charts, you should generally use not more than six components. If you have more than six, select the five components most important to your message and group the remainder into an "others" category.

Because the eye is accustomed to measuring in a clockwise motion, position the most important segment against the 12 o'clock line and, to add emphasis, use the most contrasting color (e.g., yellow against a black background), or the most intense shading pattern if producing the chart in black and white.[1] If no one segment is more important than the others, consider arranging the components from the largest to the smallest or vice versa and use either the same color or no shading for all segments.

In general, pie charts are the least practical of the five chart forms. They are also the most misused and, worse, the most abused.

For example, on the next page are several pseudo pie charts I've discovered over the years in various presentations, newspapers, magazines, and annual reports. Now I'll grant you each is imaginative and resourceful, even attractive, although example D is a bit macabre. They are also examples of form becoming more important than content and, as a result, they fail to present accurate visual relationships.

Let me stress that the primary purpose of any chart is to demonstrate relationships more quickly and more clearly than is possible using a tabular form. Whenever the form becomes more important than the content—that is, whenever the design of the chart interferes with a clear grasp of the relationship—it does a disservice to the audience or readers who may be basing decisions on the strength of what they see.

Let's have fun and do an exercise that tests the usefulness of these example as visual *aids*. To get the most from the following work project, promise that *you will not think;* record your first visual impression. For each example, starting at the top and moving down or around, quickly fill in the percentage of the total corresponding to each component. Then add the totals. Most important, you CAN'T GO BACK, you CAN'T ERASE, and fortunately you CAN'T CHANGE YOUR MIND, since you cannot think.

GO!

[1] The charts in this book are presented in black and white; they could have been shown in color as well. The use of color in business presentations and reports is discussed on page 80.

For each of these six charts, fill in the percentage you feel each segment represents and add them up.

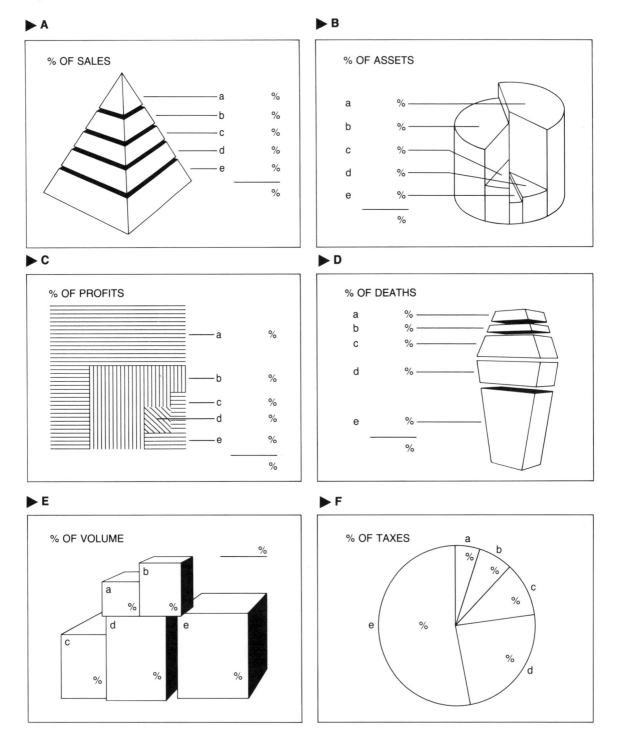

► A

% OF SALES

a ____ %
b ____ %
c ____ %
d ____ %
e ____ %
_____
____ %

► B

% OF ASSETS

a ____ %
b ____ %
c ____ %
d ____ %
e ____ %
_____
____ %

► C

% OF PROFITS

a ____ %
b ____ %
c ____ %
d ____ %
e ____ %
_____
____ %

► D

% OF DEATHS

a ____ %
b ____ %
c ____ %
d ____ %
e ____ %
_____
____ %

► E

% OF VOLUME

____ %
a ____ %
b ____ %
c ____ %
d ____ %
e ____ %

► F

% OF TAXES

a ____ %
b ____ %
c ____ %
d ____ %
e ____ %

Now compare all your guesses with the actual data that accompanied each example:

	A Percent of sales	B Percent of assets	C Percent of profits	D Percent of deaths	E Percent of volume	F Percent of taxes
a.	5%	37%	58%	7%	7%	5%
b.	7	31	32	6	15	7
c.	11	10	3	17	18	11
d.	24	14	4	16	25	24
e.	53	8	3	54	35	53
	100%	100%	100%	100%	100%	100%

If your results were radically different from these numbers—at least for Charts A through E—then it's clear that the charts are not doing the job they were intended to do, which is to give you an *accurate* impression of the relationships. I've tested these with many colleagues. Chances are your results were similar to theirs. In few cases did the data add to exactly 100 percent. Instead, the components added to less than 100 percent as often as they did to well over 100 percent. In the most extreme cases, the data added up to only 45 percent at the lower end and to 280 percent at the high end. Even when people arrived at the same total, their proportions were not necessarily similar.

On the other hand, almost everyone was accurate in estimating the percentages in Example F, *Percentage of Taxes*, presented as a conventional pie chart. Here, people could more readily *see* that segment *a* is somewhere around 5 percent and that *d* is about 25 percent, while *e* is a bit more than 50 percent. In truth, Example F is based on the same data as Example A. I just changed the titles to see what would happen. Compare the percentage values you filled in for A with those you wrote for F and note how the difference in chart form threw you off.

There's a clear lesson to be learned from this exercise: If your objective is to communicate accurate relationships, overcome the urge to be creative and instead rely on conventional pie charts. Use your creativity to make the charts attractive with handsome layouts, readable type, and constructive use of color or shadings.

A pie chart serves the purpose of showing the components of a single total better than a 100 percent bar or 100 percent column chart. However, as soon as you need to compare the components of more than one total, don't think, don't hesitate. Switch to either 100 percent bars or 100 percent columns. This example shows why.

Poor

Preferred

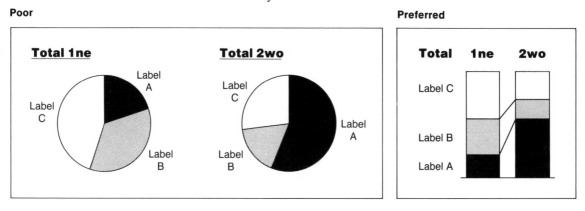

Notice how the labels must be repeated for each of the two pie charts shown. Of course, we could use a legend. However, this forces the reader to look back and forth between the legend and the components to be clear about which belongs to which. Also, although shadings—or colors—help the viewer to distinguish the three components, the eyes must travel back and forth, from pie to pie, to grasp the relationships.

By using two 100 percent columns instead, we reduce the problems. Now the labeling is less redundant, and the relationships between corresponding segments, here reinforced with connecting lines, are more quickly apparent.

2. ITEM COMPARISON

An item comparison can best be demonstrated by a bar chart.

The vertical dimension is not a scale; all it is used for is labeling the measured items—such as countries, industries, companies, salespeople's names. This being the case, you can arrange the bars in any sequence that suits the ranking you want to stress. For example, in a chart that compares the return on sales for a client company with that of its five competitors at one point in time, the bars can be sequenced by company name in alphabetical order, or by date of entry into the industry, or by size of sales, or by the magnitude of the return from either low to high or, as in this example, from high to low (from best to worst).

THE BAR CHART

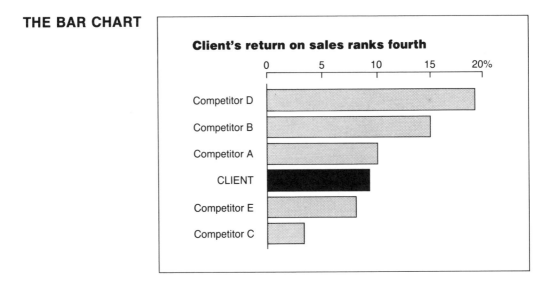

Client's return on sales ranks fourth

In preparing bar charts, make certain that the space separating the bars is smaller than the width of the bars. Use the most contrasting color or shading to emphasize the important item, thereby reinforcing the message title.

To identify the values, use either a scale at the top (sometimes at the bottom) or numbers at the ends of the bars, not both. Use the scale if all you want is a fast study of the relationships; use the numbers if they are important to your message. At times, it's a good idea to use the scale and *the one number* that needs emphasis. Using both scale and numbers, however, is redundant and adds clutter to the bar chart, as it does, for that matter, to the column chart and the line chart.

When showing numbers, round out the figures and omit decimals whenever they have little effect on your message; a figure such as 12 percent is more easily retained than 12.3 percent or 12.347 percent.

To demonstrate the versatility of the bar chart, here are six variations of the chart form, each providing additional information. Examples of the application of these variations are illustrated in Section 2 of this book. You may want to glance at them now. Certainly you will want to incorporate them into your vocabulary of charts at work.

A deviation bar chart distinguishes the profit winners from the losers

A sliding bar chart shows the different mix of two components, e.g., percentage of imports versus percentage of exports

A range bar chart shows the spread between low and high amounts, e.g., range of discounts

The paired bar chart shows the correlation between two items, e.g., growth of market versus share of market

A grouped bar chart compares various aspects of the same item, e.g., with and without discount

The subdivided bar chart shows the components that make up the total

At times, you may want to use the column chart instead of the bar chart—vertical bars instead of horizontal bars—to show an item comparison. There's really nothing violently wrong with doing so. However, 9 times out of 10, you're better off with the bar chart for two reasons. First, by reserving bar charts for showing an item comparison, we reduce the possibility of confusion with a time series comparison, for which column charts are more appropriate. To reinforce this distinction, therefore, let's avoid using the bar chart for showing changes over time; in Western culture, we're accustomed to thinking of time moving from left to right, not top to bottom.

The second reason is a practical one. Generally, items have lengthy labels—territories such as Northeast, Southwest; industries such as agriculture, manufacturing; salespeople's names—all requiring space. Notice from the two examples shown that you have all the space you need to the left of the bars to label the various items, whereas, with the column chart, you may have to go through contortions since columns are usually narrow. Here you have to squeeze the label to the point of illegibility, or hyphenate the word, or write it in an awkward manner.

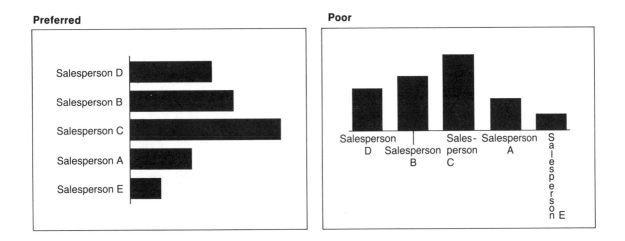

Preferred

Salesperson D
Salesperson B
Salesperson C
Salesperson A
Salesperson E

Poor

Salesperson D   Salesperson B   Sales-person C   Salesperson A   Salesperson E

3. TIME SERIES COMPARISON

Whereas a component comparison and an item comparison show relationships at one point in time, the time series comparison shows changes over time.

A time series comparison can best be demonstrated with either a column chart or a line chart. Deciding on which to use is simple. If you have only a few points in time to plot (say, up to six or seven) use the column chart; if, on the other hand, you have to show a trend over 20 years by quarters, you're much better off with the line chart.

In choosing between a column and a line chart, you can also be guided by the nature of the data. A column chart emphasizes levels or magnitudes and is more suitable for data on activities that occur within a set period of time, suggesting a fresh start for each period. Production data fit into this category. A line chart emphasizes movement and angles of change and is therefore the best form for showing data that have a "carry-over" from one time to the next. A good example here is inventory data.

Beyond these distinctions, each chart form has its own characteristics and variations, so let's study them separately.

THE COLUMN CHART

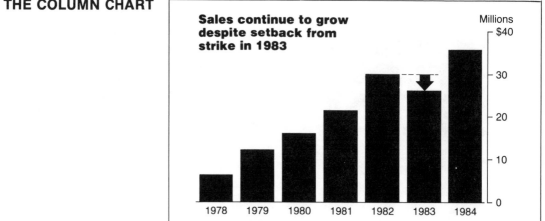

The suggestions for making the most of bar charts also apply to column charts: make the space between the columns smaller than the width of the columns; and use color or shading to emphasize one point in time more than others or to distinguish, say, historical from projected data.

As with the bar chart, there are several variations of the column chart that make it a resourceful and valuable tool; these variations are shown at work in Section 2.

	The deviation column chart distinguishes, say, the profit-making years from the losing ones.
	The range column chart shows the spread between low and high amounts, like the barometric performance of the stock market.
	The *grouped column chart,* with columns either butting against one another or overlapping, compares two items at each point in time and shows how the relationships change over time, e.g., dollars with inflation and discounted for inflation.
	A *subdivided column chart* shows how the components contributing to the total vary over time, e.g., salary plus fringe benefits adding to total compensation.
	A *step-column chart* leaves no space between the columns and is best used to show data that change abruptly at irregular intervals, such as personnel ceilings or production capacities.

THE LINE CHART

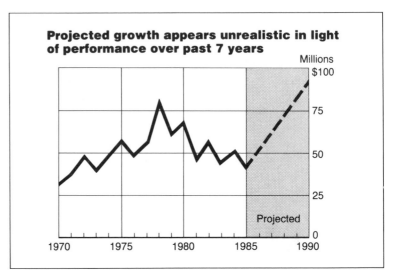

Projected growth appears unrealistic in light of performance over past 7 years

Without doubt, the line chart is the most often used of the five charts, and well it should be since it is the easiest to draw, the most compact, and the clearest for discerning whether the trend is increasing, decreasing, fluctuating, or remaining constant.

When preparing a line chart, make sure the trend line is bolder than the baseline and that the baseline, in turn, is a little bit heavier than the vertical and horizontal scale lines that shape the reference grid.

Think of grid rulings as you would the umpire at a sporting event; they're there for reference purposes, not to dominate the main attraction—in this case, the trend line(s). In other words, you may use vertical grid lines to distinguish the historic from the projected, or to emphasize quarterly periods, or to separate five-year increments. Similarly, a few horizontal scale lines will make it easier for the reader to discern relative values. In short, use your judgment to choose between too many and none at all.

The line chart has only two variations, far fewer than the bar chart or the column chart, but important enough to deserve more discussion.

The grouped line chart compares the performance of two or more items. To distinguish, say, your company's trend from those of your competitors', use the most contrasting color or the boldest solid line for your company and less intense colors or thinner or patterned lines (long dashes, short dashes) for the others.

The challenge is deciding how many trend lines we can show simultaneously before the chart looks more like spaghetti than trends. Let's be realistic, a line chart with eight trend lines isn't necessarily twice as useful as one with four lines; twice as confusing, maybe, but not twice as useful.

A technique for untangling the mess is to pair your trend with that of each competitor on a set of smaller charts, as you see. Granted, this creates more charts, but simpler comparisons per chart.

The Spaghetti Chart

Untangling the Mess

By coloring or shading the surface between the trend line and the baseline, we create the *surface chart*. By subdividing the surface into the components that make up the totals at each point in time, we create the *subdivided surface chart*. Here too, as with the subdivided bar and column charts, limit the number of layers to five or fewer. If there are more than five segments, plot only the four important ones and group the remaining into an "others" category.

For all subdivided charts, place the most important segment against the baseline, since this is the only segment that is measured against a straight line. All other segments are at the mercy of the ups and downs of that segment.

As with the spaghetti chart we just discussed, the technique for making sense of the sea of layers is to separate the components and show each on its own base, reducing the subdivided chart to simpler surface charts.

From Subdivided Line Chart

To Simpler Surface Charts

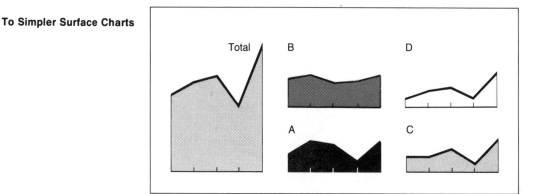

4. FREQUENCY DISTRIBUTION COMPARISON

A frequency distribution comparison shows how many items (frequency) fall into a series of progressive numerical ranges (distribution).

There are two major applications for this kind of comparison. The first is generalizing likely events on the basis of a sample of observations. Here, the frequency distribution is used to predict risk, probability, or chance. One use might be to show that there is a 25 percent chance that shipments will be delivered in five days or less; another might be to describe (un)certainty, such as the odds of rolling a losing seven, as a percentage of all possible outcomes, when shooting craps. (Save your money, the odds are one in six.)

% of all possible outcomes

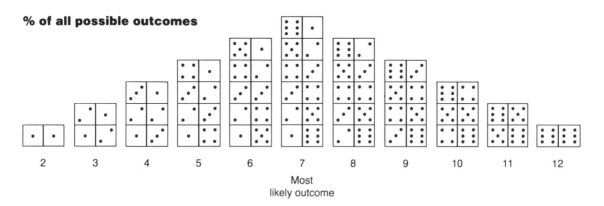

| 2 | 3 | 4 | 5 | 6 | 7 | 8 | 9 | 10 | 11 | 12 |

Most
likely outcome

The "bell-shaped" curves and frequency polygons that are associated with this application are governed by mathematical rules. Do yourself a favor and rely on the assistance of a statistician to design them. Since these "curves" are used primarily for analytical purposes, they are not our concern in this book.

The second application, often seen in business presentations and reports, is summarizing vast amounts of data to demonstrate some meaningful relationship (e.g., 25 percent of the shipments are delivered in five to six days). This application is particularly useful for demographic information such as the number of employees by salary ranges, or the distribution of U.S. families by income levels, or the voting pattern by age group. As you would expect, this use of frequency distribution gains in popularity each time the national census is taken and every four years along with presidential elections.

In this role, the frequency distribution can best be shown by either a *step-column chart (histogram)* or a *line chart (histograph)*. Column charts are better when only a few ranges are used—say, five or seven—and line charts are better when there are many.

THE COLUMN CHART (HISTOGRAM)

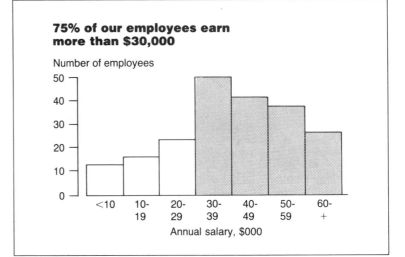

THE LINE CHART (HISTOGRAPH)

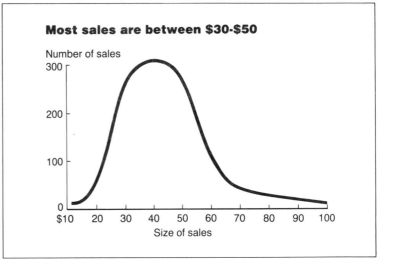

These charts have two scales: the vertical one (frequency) is for the number (sometimes percentage) of items or occurrences; the horizontal one (distribution) is for the ranges. The distribution scale requires special attention.

Size of the Ranges. The size of the ranges—and therefore the number of groups—is important in bringing out the pattern of the distribution. Too few groups hide the pattern; too many groups break it up. As a general rule, use no fewer than 5 groups and no more than 20. Within these extremes, however, you're looking for the number of groups that will demonstrate your intended message. For instance, if we wanted to bring out the pattern of a distribution of 1982 average annual salaries paid to public school teachers in the 50 states:

Grouping the ranges by $500 increments reveals no discernible pattern.

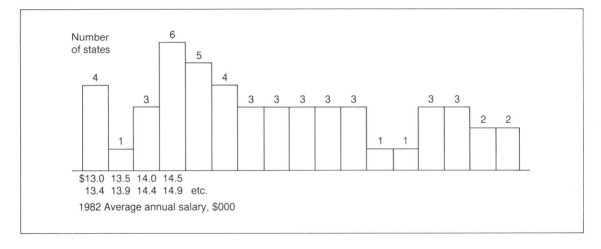

Grouping the ranges by $1,000 increments begins to suggest a pattern.

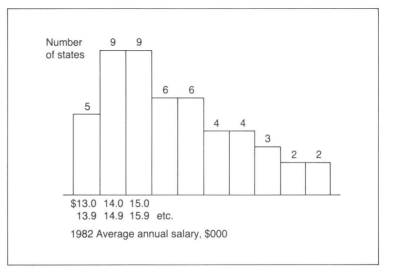

But it isn't until we group the ranges by $2,000 increments that we clearly see the bell-shaped curve usually associated with a frequency distribution. In this example, the curve is skewed to the left—that is, to the lower side of the distribution—indicating a possible message that almost half of the states (23 states out of 50) paid their teachers less than $16,000 in 1982.

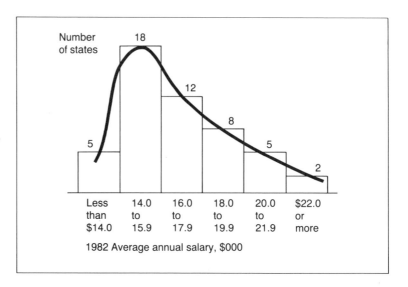

Size of the Groups. It is best to use groups of equal size. If one grouping represented a $5 range and the next, $20, the shape of the distribution would be distorted. Among the exceptions are cases where the data are not recorded in equal steps (e.g., educational levels) or where unequal steps make better sense, such as personal income tax brackets. Because the range of incomes is so great, and because there are so many people near the lower end and so few near the upper end, equal intervals won't work; $1,000 intervals would result in a chart several yards wide, $20,000 intervals would put virtually everyone in the first interval. The chart would be more informative if smaller intervals were shown at the lower end and larger ranges at the upper end.

Clear Labeling. The size of the groups should be explained clearly. "Overlapping" labels, such as 0–10, 10–20, 20–30, do not tell which groups include the repeated figure. For continuous data, such as dollar sales, the preferred method is less than $10.00, $10.00–19.99, $20.00–29.99, etc. For discrete data, such as number of cars manufactured, the preferred method is less than 10, 10–19, 20–29, etc.

Both the histogram and the histograph can be grouped to show, for instance, the distribution for one year against another, or to compare your employees' age distribution with that of a competitor or perhaps an industry average. Also, when absolute numbers are used, they can be subdivided to show how the components add to their total.[2]

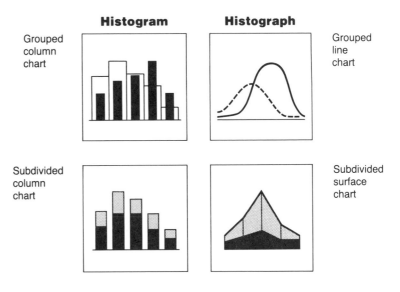

Histogram **Histograph**

Grouped column chart

Grouped line chart

Subdivided column chart

Subdivided surface chart

[2] *Caution:* It is misleading to subdivide a frequency distribution when the frequency is expressed in percentage terms. For example, if 60 percent of women earn between, say, $5 and $10 an hour, and 50 percent of men earn the same, it cannot be said that combined, 110 percent of the people earn between $5 and $10 an hour.

5. CORRELATION COMPARISON

A correlation comparison shows whether the relationship between two variables follows—or fails to follow—the pattern you would normally expect. For example, you would normally expect that a salesperson with more experience would generate more sales than one with less experience; you would normally expect that employees with more education would receive higher starting salaries. Such comparisons are best shown by a dot chart, sometimes called a scatter diagram, or by a paired bar chart. Let's look at each in turn.

THE DOT CHART

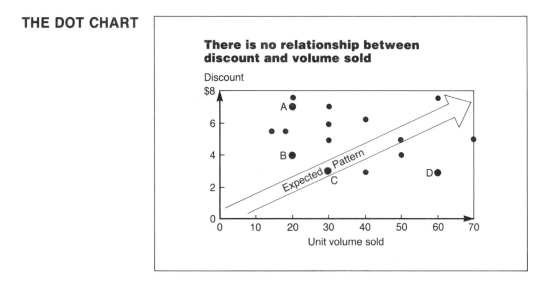

Here we show 16 transactions in terms of the size of the discount offered and the number of units sold. Normally, you would expect that the larger the discount, the greater the incentive to purchase more units. As the dot chart reveals in this case, there is no such correlation.

For instance, study the dots labeled *A* and *B*, representing the transactions of two salespeople. Both sold 20 units (horizontal scale). However, *A* offered a $7 discount, while *B* gave only $4 (vertical scale). On the other hand, salespeople *C* and *D* offered the same $3 discount, and yet *C* sold 30 units while *D* sold twice as many. Obviously, the size of the discount offered has little or no effect on the volume bought.

Had there been a correlation, then the dots would have clustered around a diagonal line moving from the lower left of the chart to the upper right, represented here by a faint background arrow. It's often a good idea to include this arrow to reinforce the expected pattern. Of course, at times, the arrow might point down to show, for example, that volume increases as price decreases. Also, let's not confuse this arrow with the mathematically computed "line of best fit," which is a curve fitted through the dots that emphasizes the pattern of the plotted values.

These dot charts are being used increasingly in presentations, reports, and some business magazines. If you plan to use them, be patient with your audience or reader and explain how to read the chart before revealing the message.

Aside from appearing confusing, the problem with these charts is identifying the dots. Including each salesperson's name next to his or her dot not only adds to the confusion but can create a severe case of myopia. An option is to use a legend with each dot identified by a letter or number corresponding to the full name shown somewhere else on the chart. A better option is to use the paired bar chart.

THE BAR CHART

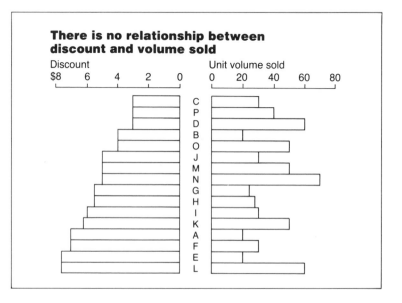

There is no relationship between discount and volume sold

Discount

$8 6 4 2 0

Unit volume sold

0 20 40 60 80

C
P
D
B
O
J
M
N
G
H
I
K
A
F
E
L

You'll notice that now there is space to label each set of plotted values between the sets of bars. In a paired bar chart, we usually rank the independent variable on the left, in either a low-to-high or high-to-low sequence. When the relationship between the expected pattern and the actual one is consistent, the dependent variable bars on the right will form a mirror image of those on the left. In other words, low discounts will mirror low volume and high discounts will be paired with high volume. When the relationship is not as expected, the two sets of bars will deviate from one another, as they do in this example.

This paired bar chart option will work only when there are relatively few sets of data to plot. Beyond 15 or so, you're better off with the more compact scatter diagram and forgetting about trying to label each dot.

While there are no variations for the paired bar chart,
there are several worth mentioning for the dot chart.

The *grouped dot chart* shows the correlation of two items
or of one item at different times. Although solid and
open dots are used here, other suitable symbols, such as
squares, triangles, or stars, can also be used.

A third variable is introduced in the *bubble chart* with
dots of different sizes. For instance, where the two
scales might represent sales and profits, the size of the
dot might indicate the relative size of assets for each
company in an industry.

The *time dot chart* shows the change over time of
the correlation. Avoid the tendency to show all
such movements on one grid; instead, place each
on its own chart.

All of the above.
A word of caution: Please keep dot charts simple
lest they become a tribute to Mickey Mouse or
Star Wars.

There you have them, the five basic kinds of comparisons implied by the messages derived from the analysis of any data, and the chart forms most appropriate for demonstrating them.

To make sure you can apply the process in actual practice, test yourself with the two work projects that follow. Afterwards, review the shopping list of charts at work in Section 2 before placing the book on your bookshelf and referring to it whenever the need arises.

WORK PROJECT A

Let's go back to the project we did at the end of Step B—identifying the comparison—and advance it to choosing the appropriate chart form for each of the 12 messages.

On the next pages are the 12 messages along with the kind of comparison you identified. Select the appropriate chart by referring to the matrix and sketch the chart you would use to support the respective messages.

As you sketch your charts, bear in mind the two important observations we've made.

1. It's not the data or the measures that indicate which chart to use; it's what *you say* about it. For instance, you'll note that for Examples 4, 6, and 7, we want to show tenure measures, and yet, for each case, we have a different comparison implied, which leads to a different chart form. So focus your attention on the trigger words, the clues in your messages. In the solutions that follow the project, these words are underlined.

2. Even without data, as we're doing here, you're able to decide which chart to use with the technique one of my colleagues called "visualizing the message, not the mess."
    The simplest test of whether a chart works is asking yourself about the finished chart: "Do I *see* what the message title *says?*" In other words, do the chart and the title work together; does the chart support the title; and does the title reinforce the chart? So, if I *say* in my title that "sales have increased significantly" I want to *see* a trend moving up at a sharp angle. If not, if the trend parallels the baseline, it's an instant clue the chart needs more thinking.

My solutions follow the messages. Don't worry if you've chosen a column chart and I show a line chart for time series comparisons or frequency distributions, or if you used the dot chart and I used a paired bar chart for correlations. In my solutions, the selection was arbitrary.

1. Sales are forecast to increase over the next 10 years **Time Series**	2. The largest number of employees earns between $20,000 and $25,000 **Frequency Distribution**
3. Higher price of gasoline brands does not indicate better performance **Correlation**	4. In September, the turnover rates for the six divisions were about the same **Item**
5. The sales manager spends only 15% of his time in the field **Component**	6. Size of merit increases is not related to tenure **Correlation**

7. Last year, most turnover was in the 30 to 35 age group
   Frequency Distribution

8. Region C ranks last in productivity
   Item

9. Our company's earnings per share is declining
   Time Series

10. The largest share of total funds is allocated to manufacturing
    Component

11. There is a relationship between profitability and compensation
    Correlation

12. In August, two plants outproduced the other six by a wide margin
    Item

1. Sales are forecast to increase over the next 10 years
   Time Series

   SALES

   PAST   NOW   NEXT 10 YEARS

2. The largest number of employees earns between $20,000 and $25,000
   Frequency Distribution

   NUMBER OF EMPLOYEES

   | LESS THAN $15.0 | 15.0 19.9 | 20.0 24.9 | 25.0 29.9 | 30.0 34.9 | 35.0 OR MORE |

   SALARY, $000

3. Higher price of gasoline brands does not indicate better performance
   Correlation

   PRICE

   BRAND
   •A
   B•
   C• D•
   E•
   F• EXPECTED •G
   •H •I

   PERFORMANCE MEASURE

4. In September, the turnover rates for the six divisions were about the same
   Item

   DIVISION   TURNOVER
   1 NE
   2 WO
   3 HREE
   4 OUR
   5 IVE
   6 IX

5. The sales manager spends only 15% of his time in the field
   Component

   % OF TOTAL TIME

   IN FIELD
   15%
   %
   SOMEWHERE ELSE
   DOING SOME OTHER THINGS
   %
   %
   DOING SOMETHING ELSE

6. Size of merit increases is not related to tenure
   Correlation

   MERIT INCREASE

   EMPLOYEE
   •A   •B
   EXPECTED

   TENURE

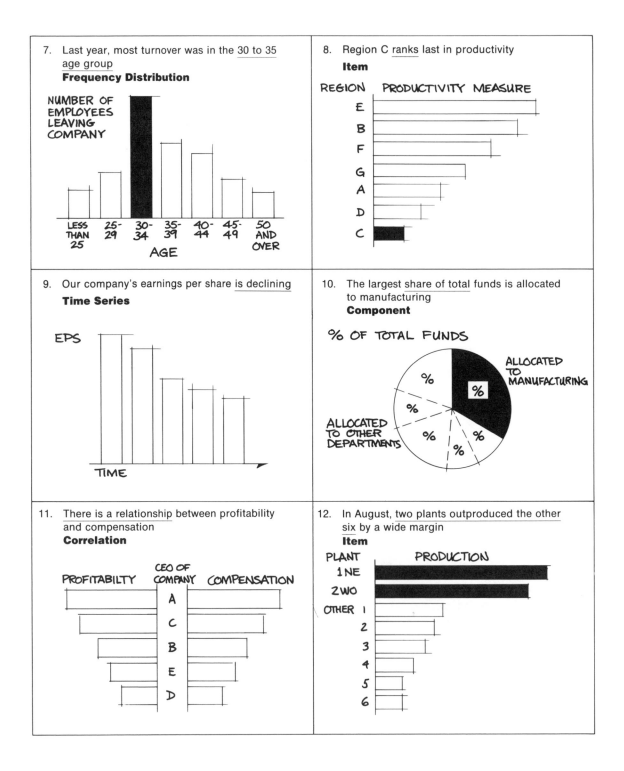

7. Last year, most turnover was in the 30 to 35 age group

Frequency Distribution

NUMBER OF EMPLOYEES LEAVING COMPANY

LESS THAN 25 | 25-29 | 30-34 | 35-39 | 40-44 | 45-49 | 50 AND OVER

AGE

8. Region C ranks last in productivity

Item

REGION | PRODUCTIVITY MEASURE

E
B
F
G
A
D
C

9. Our company's earnings per share is declining

Time Series

EPS

TIME

10. The largest share of total funds is allocated to manufacturing

Component

% OF TOTAL FUNDS

ALLOCATED TO MANUFACTURING %

ALLOCATED TO OTHER DEPARTMENTS %

11. There is a relationship between profitability and compensation

Correlation

PROFITABILTY | CEO OF COMPANY | COMPENSATION

A
C
B
E
D

12. In August, two plants outproduced the other six by a wide margin

Item

PLANT | PRODUCTION

1 NE
2 WO
OTHER 1
2
3
4
5
6

WORK PROJECT B

Now, of course, in the business world we would go through the process *with* data, so let's apply the method to one last project using tabular information.

On the following pages, you'll find several sets of data drawn from an analysis of the imagin-a-toy industry. This industry manufactures mythical toys including Slithy Toves, Gimbling Wabes, Mimsy Borogoves, Outgrabe Mome Raths, and the ever-popular Frumious Bandersnatch. The industry is made up of six competitors; ours is the Kryalot Company.

On the basis of the instructions given and the data presented, sketch the appropriate charts in the space provided. (The spaces have grids that are divided into 10 boxes to the inch to simplify plotting.)

In every instance, be sure to identify the kind of comparison the message implies and refer to the matrix to select the appropriate chart form. Also, write the message title you would use to reinforce the point each chart makes about our company.

The solution for each problem is presented on the back.

Exhibit 1

On the basis of the following data, sketch a chart to demonstrate Kryalot's share of imagin-a-toy industry sales in 1984 compared with that of our competitors'.

Share of Industry Sales By Company, 1984

Kryalot	19.3%
Competitor A	10.1%
Competitor B	16.6%
Competitor C	12.4%
Competitor D	31.8%
Competitor E	9.8%
	100.0%

SOLUTION

For Exhibit 1, the phrase "share of 1984 industry sales" serves as the clue to a component comparison—the size of the parts as a percentage of the total—and calls for a pie chart since we're speaking about a single total.

Here, the components have been arranged clockwise, proceeding from the company with the largest share to the company with the smallest, thereby positioning Kry-alot as having the second-largest share. To emphasize Kryalot's share, we used the shading for that segment.

Exhibit 1

KRYALOT HAS THE SECOND-LARGEST SHARE OF INDUSTRY SALES IN 1984

COMPETITOR E — 9.8%
COMPETITOR A — 10.1%
COMPETITOR C — 12.4%
COMPETITOR D — 31.8%
16.6%
19.3% — KRYALOT
COMPETITOR B

Exhibit 2

Sketch a chart that demonstrates how Kryalot's return on assets ranks in the industry in 1984.

Return on Assets, 1984

Kryalot	8.3%
Competitor A	9.8%
Competitor B	15.9%
Competitor C	22.4%
Competitor D	14.7%
Competitor E	19.1%

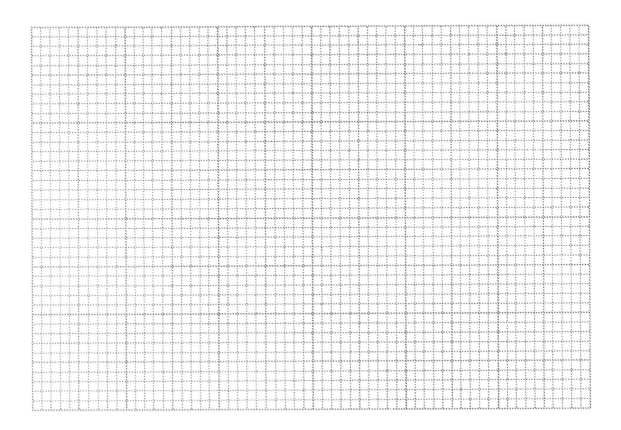

SOLUTION

In Exhibit 2, the word "rank" is the trigger that implies an item comparison. Here, we want to know which competitor has the highest return on assets and which has the lowest. In this case, Kryalot has the lowest. Notice how the bar chart effectively demonstrates the point by positioning Kryalot at the bottom of the list and emphasizing it once more with the darkest shading.

Exhibit 2

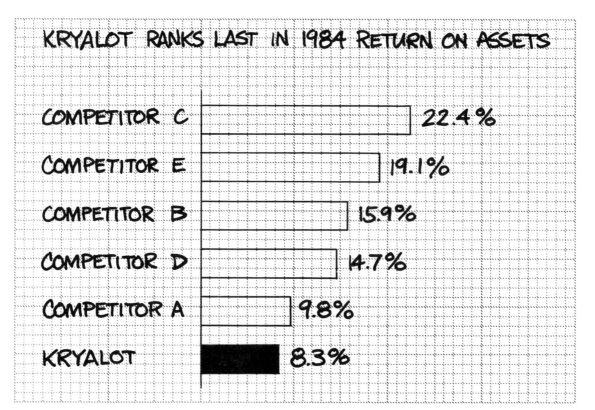

KRYALOT RANKS LAST IN 1984 RETURN ON ASSETS

COMPETITOR C	22.4%
COMPETITOR E	19.1%
COMPETITOR B	15.9%
COMPETITOR D	14.7%
COMPETITOR A	9.8%
KRYALOT	8.3%

Exhibit 3

Sketch a chart that demonstrates whether a relationship exists between share of sales and return on assets in the imagin-a-toy industry in 1984.

Share of Industry Sales, 1984

Kryalot	19.3%
Competitor A	10.1%
Competitor B	16.6%
Competitor C	12.4%
Competitor D	31.8%
Competitor E	9.8%

Return on Assets, 1984

Kryalot	8.3%
Competitor A	9.8%
Competitor B	15.9%
Competitor C	22.4%
Competitor D	14.7%
Competitor E	19.1%

SOLUTION

We would normally expect a relationship between share of sales and return on assets; that is, the greater the share, the higher the return. Here, the data indicate this is not so. For instance, although Kryalot has the second-largest share, it has a return much lower than that of, say, Competitor C, which ranks fourth in its share of market.

Although the dot chart would be equally appropriate, the paired bar chart allows us to label each set of paired bars more effectively.

Exhibit 3

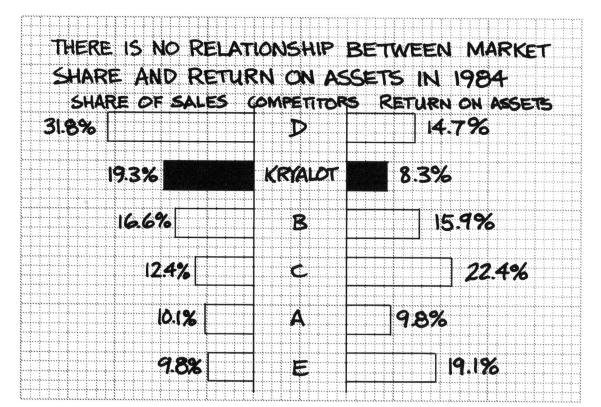

THERE IS NO RELATIONSHIP BETWEEN MARKET SHARE AND RETURN ON ASSETS IN 1984

SHARE OF SALES	COMPETITORS	RETURN ON ASSETS
31.8%	D	14.7%
19.3%	KRYALOT	8.3%
16.6%	B	15.9%
12.4%	C	22.4%
10.1%	A	9.8%
9.8%	E	19.1%

64

Exhibit 4

Sketch a chart that demonstrates the trends for Kryalot's sales and earnings between 1980 and 1984, using 1980 as the base year and showing succeeding years as a percentage of the base year.

Kryalot Net Sales

	$ Millions	1980 = 100
1980	$387	100
1981	420	109
1982	477	123
1983	513	133
1984	530	137

Kryalot Earnings

	$ Millions	1980 = 100
1980	$24	100
1981	39	162
1982	35	146
1983	45	188
1984	29	121

SOLUTION

Exhibit 4 calls for demonstrating changes over time—a time series comparison—and the line chart serves the purpose well.

We translated the absolute data into percentages of a base value—in this case 1980 figures—to provide a common, and clearer, basis for comparison of disparate figures: $530 million as compared to $29 million.

This is an excellent example of the value charts have over tabular data. The chart clearly demonstrates the erratic pattern of earnings, which might not have been as obvious had the data been left in tabular form.

Exhibit 4

SINCE 1980, KRYALOT SALES HAVE BEEN RISING STEADILY WHILE EARNINGS HAVE BEEN FLUCTUATING

INDEX: 1980 = 100

200
175
150
125
100

1980 1981 1982 1983 1984

— SALES
EARNINGS

Exhibit 5

Sketch a chart demonstrating that in 1984 most of our sales, unlike those of Competitor D, are for the less expensive models of Frumious Bandersnatch.

	Number of Units Sold, 000	
Size of Sales	Kryalot	Competitor D
Less than $5.00	320	280
$ 5.00–$ 9.99	770	340
$10.00–$14.99	410	615
$15.00–$19.99	260	890
$20.00 or more	105	550

SOLUTION

Exhibit 5 calls for a frequency distribution comparison, that is, the number of units that are sold in particular price ranges. In this case, we displayed the column chart for Kryalot against the stepped column chart for Competitor D. Two superimposed lines could also have been shown but, with so few data points, the columns are preferable.

Exhibit 5

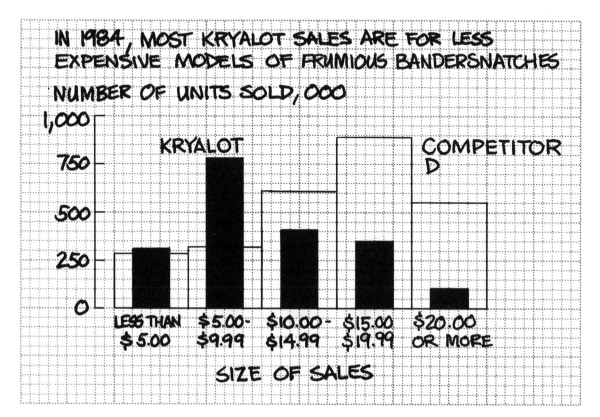

IN 1984, MOST KRYALOT SALES ARE FOR LESS EXPENSIVE MODELS OF FRUMIOUS BANDERSNATCHES

NUMBER OF UNITS SOLD, 000

KRYALOT

COMPETITOR D

LESS THAN $5.00 / $5.00-$9.99 / $10.00-$14.99 / $15.00-$19.99 / $20.00 OR MORE

SIZE OF SALES

Exhibit 6

Sketch a chart that demonstrates how our product sales mix differs from that of Competitor D's in 1984.

Percentage of Total Sales by Product, 1984

Products	Kryalot	Competitor D
Slithy Toves	15.0%	25.3%
Gimbling Wabes	8.4%	21.3%
Mimsy Borogoves	20.6%	19.9%
Outgrabe Mome Raths	16.2%	18.6%
Frumious Bandersnatches	39.8%	14.9%
	100.0%	100.0%

SOLUTION

In this last exhibit, we're back where we started with a component comparison—that is, showing percentage of total sales. As the matrix indicates, we could use pie charts. However, since we're dealing with more than one total, one for Kryalot *and* one for Competitor D, we're better off with 100 percent columns. This avoids the redundant labels that would have to be used with two pies, eliminates the need for a legend, and gives us a chart that more quickly demonstrates the relationships between the segments.

Exhibit 6

IN 1984, KRYALOT'S PRODUCT MIX DIFFERS
FROM THAT OF COMPETITOR D'S

	KRYALOT 100%	COMPETITOR D 100%
GIMBLING WABES	8.4%	21.3%
SLITHY TOVES	15.0%	
OUTGRABE MOME RATHS	16.2%	25.3%
MIMSY BOROGOVES	20.6%	18.6%
FRUMIOUS BANDERSNATCHES	39.8%	19.7%
		14.9%

Let me summarize the major messages presented thus far.

¶ Charts are an important form of language. When well conceived and designed, they help you communicate more quickly and more clearly than you can with the data in tabular form.

¶ It's neither the data nor the measures that indicate what form of chart to use; it's *your* message, what *you* want to show, the specific point *you* want to make.

¶ Fewer is better. Use charts only when they will clearly help to get your message across.

¶ Charts are visual *aids;* they are not a substitute for writing or saying what you mean. Help them help you get your message across, and they'll serve you well.

USING
CHARTS

Following is a portfolio of 80 charts at work. The charts are organized around the five basic kinds of comparison: component, item, time series, frequency distribution, and correlation. The time series section is further subdivided into a segment each for column charts, line charts, and combinations of column and line charts. Within each section, the charts are presented in increasing order of complexity ranging from, say, one pie per chart to multiple pies.

MESSAGE TITLES

To reinforce Step 1 in the process of choosing charts, *message titles* are included for all the examples. In actual practice, you might want to delete them from the charts. For example, when producing 35mm slides where space is limited, you might decide to include the message title only in your written script and not show it on the slide. However, omitting the title does not mean omitting the step of making certain, first and foremost, that *you* are clear about *your* message, what *you* want to show, the specific point *you* want to make, since this will determine the chart form to use.

DUAL COMPARISONS

For some of the examples, you will note that the charts look suspiciously as if they should belong in another segment. This was done because, at times, the *message* you have determined, based upon your analysis of the data, will imply a *dual* comparison, e.g., item and component or time series and item. In these cases, you must determine which comparison is primary and which is secondary. Consider, for example, the following message which contains both a time series and an item comparison: "Sales are forecast to increase over the next 10 years, but profits may not keep pace." The first part of the message is a time series comparison. But with the statement, "but profits may not keep pace," we add a second, item, comparison. In other words, we are interested not only in the chronological change in sales (time series) but also in the performance of sales (item number 1) compared with profits (item number 2). However, the primary emphasis remains on changes over time, and we would therefore use the basic chart form most appropriate to a time series comparison. In this case, the best choice would be a line chart with a separate line for each of the two items. In the portfolio, these dual comparison charts have been included in the section on the comparison I judged to be primary.

SCALES

Scale values have been omitted since the nature and magnitude of the data being plotted (e.g., sales dollars in thousands) is not important for our purposes in this portfolio. Naturally, scale values are used in practice, but omitting them should not obscure the relationship each chart illustrates. In fact, it is a good test of your own charts to see whether messages come across clearly without showing the scales.

This does not mean that scaling considerations are unimportant to the design of charts.[1] On the contrary, the wrong scale can lead to producing a chart that is misleading or worse, dishonest. Here is an extreme example of each.

[1] For a more thorough presentation of the misuse and abuse of scales, refer to my article, "Grappling with Graphics," *Management Review*, October 1975. The selected examples presented in this section are reprinted, with the permission of the publisher, from MANAGEMENT REVIEW, October 1975 © 1975 by AMACOM, a division of American Management Associations, New York. All rights reserved.

EXAMPLE ▶ 1

Misleading   **Accurate**

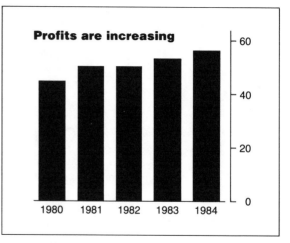

In Example 1, the chart at the left shows a picture of the trend in profits for the past five years. Our quick impression is that profits are declining. However, on closer inspection we notice four scaling problems: (1) the years are shown in reverse, moving from the most recent year at the left to earlier years at the right (a carry-over from annual reports, in which the most recent annual data are placed at the left to attract more immediate attention); (2) the bottom 20 units of profits are lopped off; (3) the columns are in three dimensions, so it's hard to know whether to measure their height from the front or the rear; (4) the scale lines are drawn in perspective. Together they create an unfortunately misleading picture of declining performance. Pity the shareholders.

In the chart at the right, we see more quickly and clearly that profits are increasing.

EXAMPLE ▶ 2

Dishonest   **Accurate**

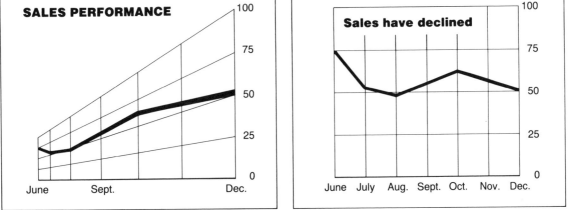

In the second example, foreshortening the scale lines in the chart on the left produces the impression that sales are increasing. Not true, as we can see from the chart on the right.

The point is this: a chart is a picture of relationships, and only the picture counts. Everything else—titles, labels, scale values—merely identifies and explains. The most important feature of the picture is the *impression* you receive. Scaling has an important controlling effect on that impression. Here is a demonstration of how easily and how substantially the scale can shape your impression of the message. Which would you choose, A or B?

▶ A

▶ B

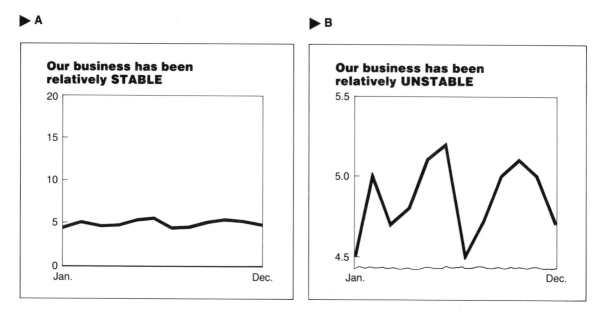

Our business has been relatively STABLE

Our business has been relatively UNSTABLE

It would be easy to opt for the answer: "Something in between," and yet that, too, may be inappropriate. The decision rests on *your professional understanding of the significance of the changes.* And so, a $1,000 change in a multimillion contract may be insignificant while a one-cent change in the price of a floor tile may be. You would therefore select a scale to reflect your understanding of the importance of the changes; perhaps the picture at the left would be appropriate for contracts, the one at the right for floor tiles.

To provide an accurate impression of your understanding of the changes, construct your charts with a respect for the factors that influence the picture:

The shape of the chart, from short and wide to tall and narrow

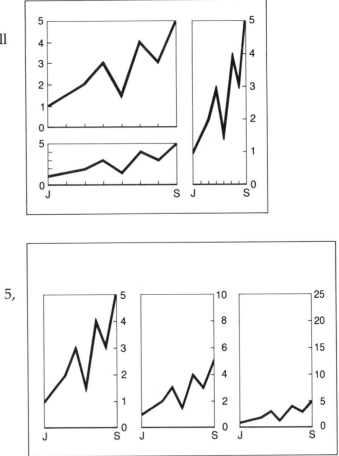

The scale range, say, 0 to 5, 0 to 10, or 0 to 25

These and other important scaling considerations are discussed in the commentary that accompanies each chart in the portfolio.

COLOR

Note that the charts in the portfolio—and throughout the book—achieve the desired visual impact in black and white. If you choose to use color in your business presentations and reports, keep the following thoughts in mind:

¶ *First*, if the charts do not communicate in black and white, color is not going to help. A good test of your charts (along with omission of scales) is to see whether messages come across quickly and clearly without using color.

¶ *Second*, for many business presentations, the use of color can suggest frivolous expense, especially if the focus of the presentation is to cut costs.

¶ *Third*, the technology for making color paper copies from color slides or transparencies doesn't quite meet management needs. The current technology is more expensive than we like, slower than we need, or provides a lower quality than we want.

Certainly, this is not to suggest that color should never be used; color can add impact, capture interest, focus attention. However, use color not just to decorate, but for a purpose:

¶ *To emphasize*—e.g., one component of a pie, one segment of a bar or column, a trend line, a row of figures, words in a title.

¶ *To identify a recurring theme*—e.g., showing company-related data in the same color in all charts.

¶ *To distinguish*—e.g., actual from projected, one set of bars or columns from another, one trend line from another.

¶ *To symbolize*—e.g., red for losses; red for stop, yellow for proceed with caution, and green for go.

One final word of caution: All charts in this book are derived from fictitious data. They are for illustrative purposes only and must not be used as source material for content.

COMPONENT COMPARISON

*Shows the size of each part as
a percentage of the total*

COMPONENT COMPARISON

 1

Chart 1 illustrates the simplest—and only truly appropriate—use of the pie chart: to compare a few components. Four shadings are used to distinguish the companies, with the darkest shading reserved for Company A to emphasize the aspect of the data mentioned in the title.

2

Chart 2 illustrates two methods of focusing attention on a component: (1) using darker shading; and (2) separating the segment from the remainder of the pie. In this example, the components are arranged according to the natural flow of activities.

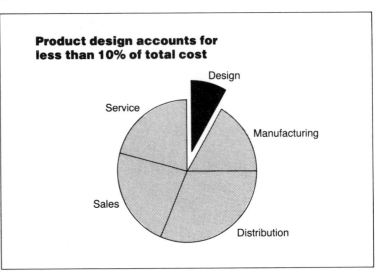

Product design accounts for less than 10% of total cost

Because the eye tends to complete the circumference of a circle, omitting a segment draws attention to the missing component, as Chart 3 shows. In this case, the lack of effort in recruiting new business is implied by the omission of the segment. The arrow further draws your attention to the sector.

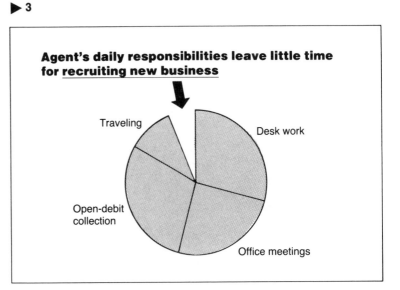

Agent's daily responsibilities leave little time for recruiting new business

▶ 4

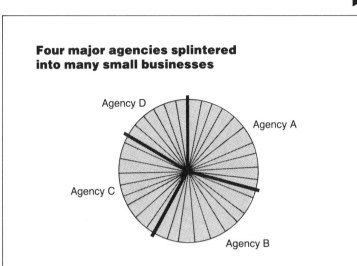

Four major agencies splintered into many small businesses

Agency D

Agency A

Agency C

Agency B

Although Chart 4 violates the guideline against using more than six components in a pie chart, it is used in this case to emphasize the message that there are many agency businesses. Note that it is virtually impossible to measure the relative size of each component; if you must do so, you are better off presenting the data in tabular form or as a bar chart (see Charts 12 and 13).

▶ 5

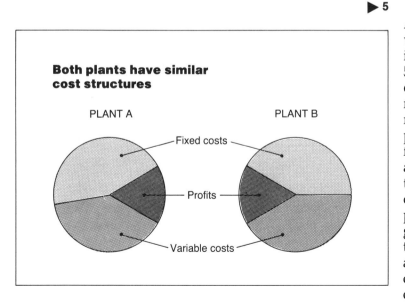

Both plants have similar cost structures

PLANT A

PLANT B

Fixed costs

Profits

Variable costs

Arranging the components within each pie in a mirror image, as is done in Chart 5, permits the use of only one set of labels. This makes it unnecessary to repeat the labels for each pie or to use a legend that forces you to look back and forth from the legend to the respective component. In the process, we disregard two guidelines: (1) starting at the 12 o'clock baseline; and (2) arranging the components in the same order.

Chart 6 compares components within separate pies. When using this technique, keep things simple—no more than three components, no more than two pies. Beyond two pies, it is better to switch to 100 percent columns (see Chart 40).

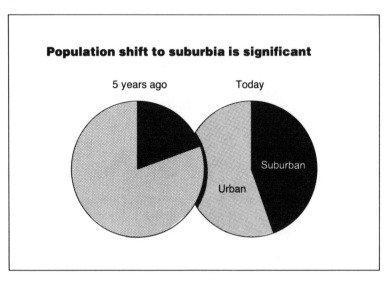

Population shift to suburbia is significant

5 years ago   Today

Urban   Suburban

I hesitate to include Chart 7, since it will work only with two components, and even then the shading may be confusing. On the other hand, when kept simple, as we see here, it can be memorable. If in doubt, do not hesitate and use the more conventional two sets of 100 percent columns.

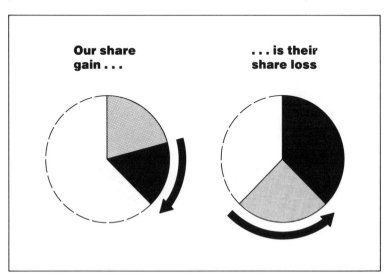

Our share gain . . .   **. . . is their share loss**

▶ 8

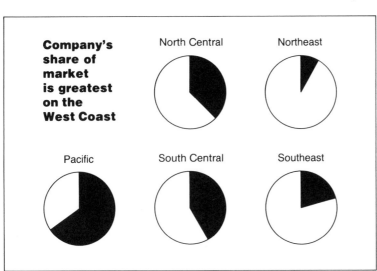

By using a separate pie for each region, as in Chart 8, we see: first, the company's share in each region; and second, the variation from region to region. Although 100 percent bars (see Chart 21) could be used, positioning the pies to simulate the natural geographic location makes this presentation more effective.

▶ 9

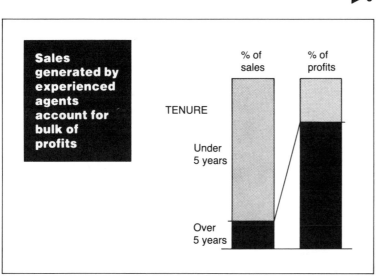

Chart 9 illustrates that, as soon as you need to show the relationship among components for more than one total, you are better off with either 100 percent bars or 100 percent columns. Commonly referred to as the 20/80 chart, this chart demonstrates that, although the more experienced agents account for the smallest share of sales, they concentrate on those sales that generate the larger share of profits.

You can show more than two items and two components per item in a 100 percent column chart, as Chart 10 indicates, but you should avoid using more than three of each because it may become confusing to follow this kind of comparison. Charts 9 and 10 could be shown with horizontal rather than vertical bars. However, the arrangements shown have become widely used and accepted.

 10

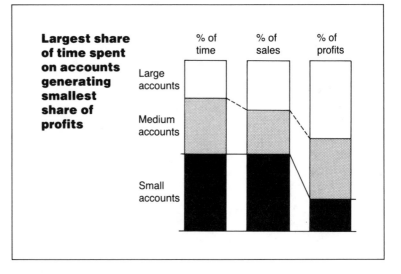

Largest share of time spent on accounts generating smallest share of profits

Large accounts

Medium accounts

Small accounts

% of time

% of sales

% of profits

▶ 11

Chart 11 combines a pie chart and a 100 percent column to permit comparison of a total within a total: (1) of total employees, the percentage who are under 30 years old; and (2) of those under 30, the percentage distribution by education level.

When using this combination, always start with the pie chart and follow with the 100 percent column, not the other way around.

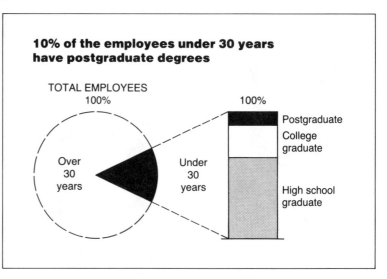

10% of the employees under 30 years have postgraduate degrees

TOTAL EMPLOYEES
100%

Over 30 years

Under 30 years

100%

Postgraduate

College graduate

High school graduate

ITEM COMPARISON

Shows ranking of items

ITEM COMPARISON

▶ 12

In a bar chart, such as Chart 12, the order of the items can be important. In this presentation, the items are sequenced from high to low to provide a ranking from best to worst performance and to show where the client ranks in the lineup. The client's return on sales has been highlighted by using a darker shading and a different type style for the label.

Client's return on sales ranks fourth

Competitor D

Competitor B

Competitor A

CLIENT

Competitor E

Competitor C

Instead of ranking the items from high to low or vice versa, Chart 13 uses a haphazard arrangement to emphasize the unevenness of salespersons' performance mentioned in the message title.

Sales performance is uneven

Sales rep. D

Sales rep. B

Sales rep. F

Sales rep. A

Sales rep. E

Sales rep. C

▶ 14

Chart 14 places the labels above instead of beside the bars. In this case, better use is made of the vertical space, permitting a smarter-looking and more compact layout. In the process, more space for the horizontal scale is provided to stress the important differences between departments.

Turnover rates vary by department

Research and Development

Manufacturing

Marketing

Distribution

▶ 15

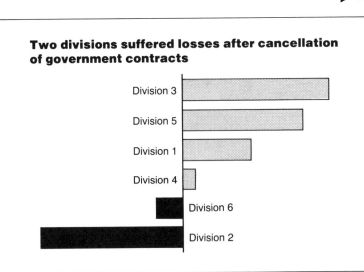

Two divisions suffered losses after cancellation of government contracts

- Division 3
- Division 5
- Division 1
- Division 4
- Division 6
- Division 2

Chart 15 is a deviation bar chart in which bars extended to the left of the baseline—like columns extended below the zero line—suggest unfavorable results or conditions. The vertical baseline separates the profitable divisions from the losers. The items are ranked from most profitable to least profitable. To keep the chart compact, the labels are shifted from the left for profits to the right for losses.

▶ 16

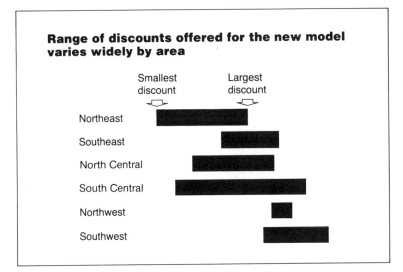

Range of discounts offered for the new model varies widely by area

Smallest discount   Largest discount

- Northeast
- Southeast
- North Central
- South Central
- Northwest
- Southwest

Chart 16, a range bar chart, shows the spread between low and high amounts, rather than just the single amounts. Range bars are useful when interest is in the amounts at each end of the range as well as in the difference between them.

Chart 17 is a bar chart in which two or more sets of bars can be compared, providing for both vertical and horizontal comparison. Of the two comparisons, the vertical one is more direct because the items are measured against a common baseline, while it is more difficult to compare the items horizontally, since they do not stack against the same baseline. Although the averages could have been shown as bars, the dashed lines that cut across each company's performance distinguish more clearly those sales that are above the average from those that are below.

▶ 17

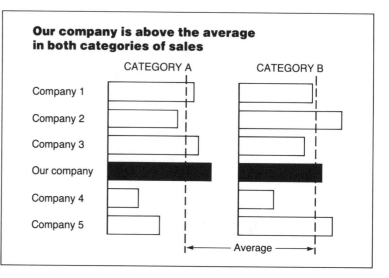

Chart 18 is a grouped bar chart that compares a number of items—Plants 1, 2, 3—at two points in time. Different shadings are used to distinguish time periods. The dashed lines and arrows, although not necessary, help to emphasize the direction and amount of change.

▶ 18

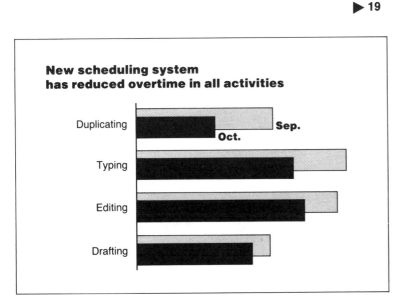

▶ 19

**New scheduling system
has reduced overtime in all activities**

Chart 19 is a special form of grouped bar chart that is sometimes effective. Overlapping the bars saves vertical space, helps to emphasize the more recent time period, and focuses attention on the gap between the two time periods. In this example, the activities are listed by the decreasing size of the gap. They could also have been arranged by the normal flow of activities; i.e., from editing to typing to drafting to duplicating. Note: this technique is effective only if the bar in the background is consistently longer than the one in the foreground. If it is not, the background bar appears thinner than the foreground bar and may confuse the viewer.

Charts 18 and 19 disregard the guideline against using bar charts to show changes over time. It works here with only two time periods. With more than two, use column charts.

Chart 20 is a subdivided bar chart in which the bars and their components are plotted according to absolute rather than relative values—that is, in dollars, tons, customers, or some other direct unit of measurement instead of in percentages.

Note that for all subdivided bar, column, and line charts, you should put the most important component against the baseline, since only the components against the base can be compared accurately.

Chart 21 is a 100 percent subdivided bar chart in which each bar and its components are plotted according to the relative (percentage) size of its components regardless of the absolute total value represented by the bar. In this type of chart, there are two baselines against which to place the important components—the one at the left which connects the bars, and the one at the right which is not connected.

▶ 20

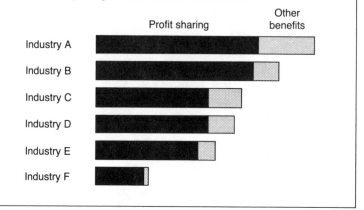

Although total fringe benefits vary, profit sharing is the largest portion in all industries

▶ 21

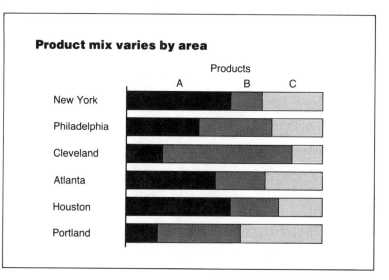

Product mix varies by area

▶ 22

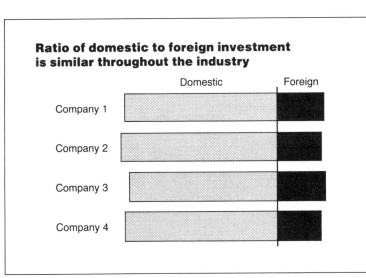

Ratio of domestic to foreign investment is similar throughout the industry

Domestic · Foreign

Company 1
Company 2
Company 3
Company 4

Chart 22 is a sliding subdivided bar chart, useful when there are only two components (or two major groups of components). Because the dividing line between the two segments serves as a common baseline, each component can be compared accurately. In this case the bars are 100 percent, although absolute values can also be used.

▶ 23

PVC has penetrated the market

PVC · Carpet · Other
Flooring

PVC · Steel · Other
Pipe

PVC · Polyethylene · Other
Wire and cable

Charts 23 through 27 introduce the use of arrows in bar charts. Although not necessary, the arrows add a sense of direction and movement that can often add emphasis to the message title.

Chart 23 is, like Chart 21, a subdivided 100 percent bar chart. Here, however, the arrows used to show PVC's share accent the idea of penetration mentioned in the title.

▶ 24

Chart 24 can prove valuable for visualizing the highlights of a profit and loss statement. The components of assets are built up to their cumulative total and balanced against the components of liabilities. Certainly the bars could be vertical instead of horizontal, although the treatment used here provides more room to the left of the bars for labeling the components.

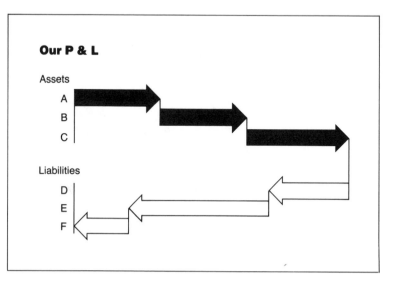

Our P & L

Assets

A
B
C

Liabilities

D
E
F

▶ 25

Chart 25 has become known as a source of change chart. The solid arrows show the cost that is *added* at each successive stage of a process; the lighter segments indicate the carry-over from the previous stages.

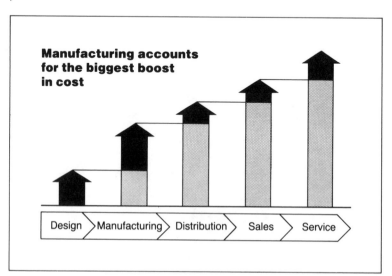

Manufacturing accounts for the biggest boost in cost

Design   Manufacturing   Distribution   Sales   Service

▶ **26**

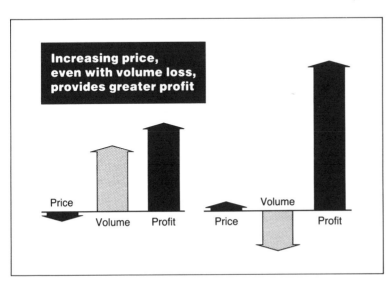

Sensitivity analyses are often demonstrated using the treatment shown in Chart 26. This deviation chart stresses the impact on profits of various changes in one or more related items. Here, use of dynamic arrows, rather than static bars, emphasizes the nature of the changes, both positive and negative.

▶ **27**

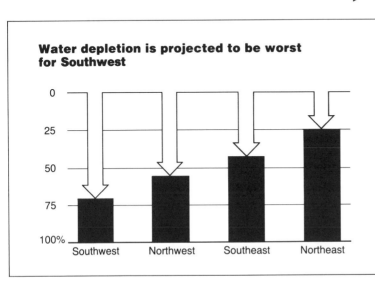

Chart 27 works well in spite of—or perhaps because of—the unconventional treatment of the scale, which begins at the top with 0 percent and moves down to 100 percent. The arrows stress the magnitude of the depletion while pointing to the percentage that remains. The items have been ranked beginning with the region most affected by the depletion and progressing to the region least affected.

Chart 28 combines a pie chart, which summarizes the total picture, with a bar chart, which itemizes the reasons salespeople are leaving their current company. The solid bar focuses attention on the fact that most are leaving to take on similar positions with other companies, indicating a problem with their position in this company.

▶ 28

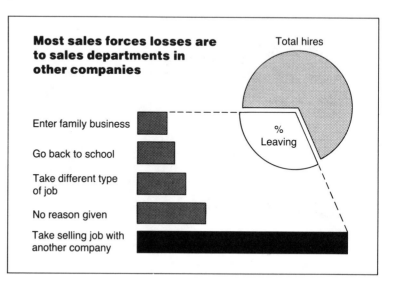

Most sales forces losses are to sales departments in other companies

Total hires

Enter family business

Go back to school

Take different type of job

No reason given

Take selling job with another company

% Leaving

TIME SERIES COMPARISON

Shows changes over time

TIME SERIES COMPARISON
COLUMN CHARTS

▶ 29

Chart 29 is a simple column chart suitable for showing changing levels over time. The column chart is best used for fewer than seven time periods.

Use graphic treatments—arrows, lines, shadings, or color—when you want to emphasize a specific aspect of the data, as shown here and on the next three charts. In this presentation, the arrow serves the dual purpose of focusing attention on the year 1983 and emphasizing the downward level.

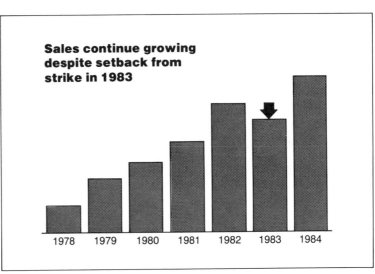

Sales continue growing despite setback from strike in 1983

1978 1979 1980 1981 1982 1983 1984

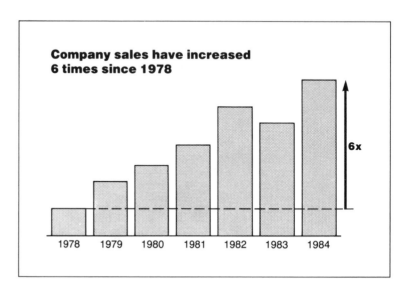

▶ 30

In Chart 30, the arrow emphasizes the increase from 1978 through 1984.

Company sales have increased 6 times since 1978

1978 1979 1980 1981 1982 1983 1984

6x

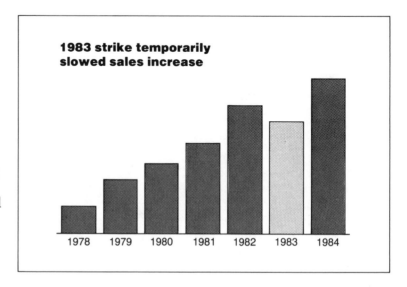

▶ 31

Chart 31 uses lighter shading for 1983 to distinguish that year from all others. This treatment emphasizes how much sales *were* in 1983, rather than how much *less* they were than in 1982. This use of dark and light shading can also prove effective for distinguishing actual from estimated data or historical from projected data.

1983 strike temporarily slowed sales increase

1978 1979 1980 1981 1982 1983 1984

► 32

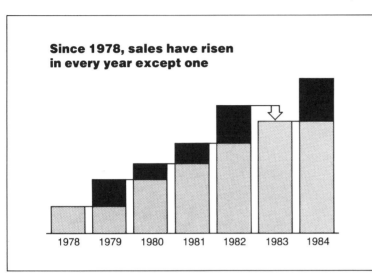

**Since 1978, sales have risen
in every year except one**

| 1978 | 1979 | 1980 | 1981 | 1982 | 1983 | 1984 |

Chart 32 combines graphic treatments—darker column caps and an arrow—to highlight the amount of change from year to year and to distinguish between periods of growth and the period of decline.

► 33

**New management team has successfully
turned losses into profits**

1976 1977 1978 1979 1980   1981   1982   1983   1984

Chart 33 employs several techniques to distinguish between positive and negative data: (1) extending columns below the zero line to indicate deficits or unfavorable conditions; (2) using different shadings; and (3) staggering the column labels.

▶ 34

Chart 34 is on the page of our daily newspaper when we study the performance of the stock market. It is a range column chart and emphasizes the spread between two sets of values—in this case, the daily high and low—rather than just the magnitude of the values. The crossline, generally used to indicate the average of the high/low values, here indicates the closing level for each day.

What goes up . . . must come down

High
Close
Low

M T W T F   M T W T F
Week 1   Week 2

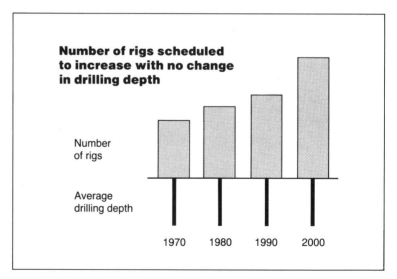

▶ 35

Chart 35 butts two column charts on either side of the baseline: above, the columns indicate the increasing number of rigs; below, they show the average depth the rigs drill into the earth. In this case, the columns extended below the line indicate neither a deficit nor an unfavorable condition, but instead reinforce the idea of depth; also, the columns have been narrowed to suggest drilling bits.

Number of rigs scheduled to increase with no change in drilling depth

Number of rigs

Average drilling depth

1970   1980   1990   2000

▶ 36

Five-year objectives call for substantial increases in stores, revenues, and profits

Number of stores

Revenues ($ millions)

Profits ($ millions)

Chart 36 is a grouped column chart for three sets of data that are measured in different kinds of units (number of stores versus dollars) and in different sized units (revenues in $ hundred millions versus profits in $ ten millions). To provide a common base of comparison, translate the absolute data into percentages (or an index) of the base value (in this case, 1989 divided by 1984) and plot the 1984 base values at equal heights. In other words, we assume that in 1984 the number of stores equaled the revenues and the profits. Then plot the 1989 values according to their percentage increase. The result is a "visual" index chart that allows you to show the absolute values while plotting the percentage changes in proportion to one another.

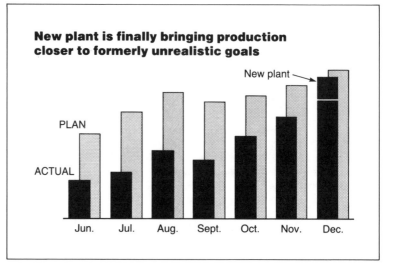

▶ 37

New plant is finally bringing production closer to formerly unrealistic goals

New plant

PLAN

ACTUAL

Jun.   Jul.   Aug.   Sept.   Oct.   Nov.   Dec.

Overlapping columns, as in Chart 37, works well when the two items are related aspects of the same measurement. In this case, the two items—planned versus actual—are related aspects of production. (Remember, one item should be consistently greater than the other. Otherwise the overlapping column hides the thickness of the column in the background.)

▶ 38

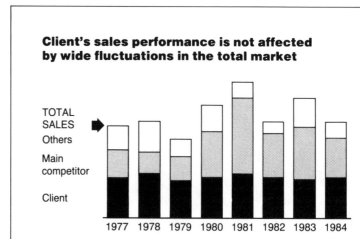

Client's sales performance is not affected by wide fluctuations in the total market

TOTAL
SALES
Others

Main
competitor

Client

1977   1978   1979   1980   1981   1982   1983   1984

Chart 38 is a subdivided column chart that shows how the totals change over time and the components contribute to the change. For all subdivided charts, the tendency is to show too many components, making individual segments difficult to identify and compare. Use not more than five. If you need accurate measurements of each component, rely on the approach illustrated by the next chart.

▶ 39

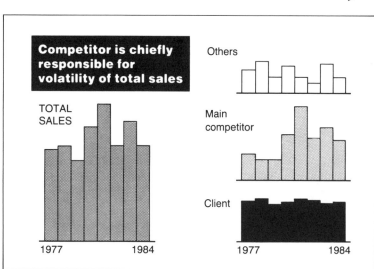

Chart 39 employs the same data used in Chart 38 but presents them in such a way that the trends for the total and for each component can be measured accurately against its own baseline. This alters the focus of the chart from how the components contribute to the changing trend over time to how each item varies over time.

▶ 40

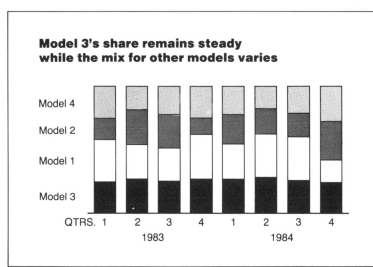

Chart 40 is a 100 percent subdivided column chart. Although the eye is accustomed to reading a page from top to bottom, a column chart is measured from the zero line up (as is a subdivided surface chart). For this reason, the most important component is usually positioned against that base. Use different shadings to distinguish the components within the columns and to help identify the pattern of change for each component across the chart.

Chart 41 is a column chart that indicates the source of change from the volume at the beginning of the time period to the volume at the end. Here, arrows reinforce the positive and negative nature of the changes while measuring the amounts of change each account represents.

▶ 41

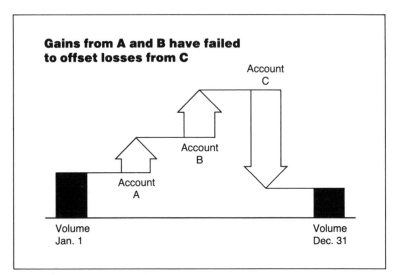

Gains from A and B have failed to offset losses from C

Account C

Account B

Account A

Volume Jan. 1

Volume Dec. 31

▶ 42

Chart 42, a step-column chart, could be thought of as a column chart with no space between the columns or as a surface (line) chart with the space between the line and the base shaded; without the shading, it becomes a line chart. It is best for presentation of data that change abruptly at irregular intervals, such as staffing levels.

A higher production plateau has been reached since introduction of new equipment in early 1984

Volume

| Qtrs. 2 | 3 | 4 | 1 | 2 | 3 | 4 | 1 | 2 | 3 | 4 |
| 1982 | | | 1983 | | | | 1984 | | | |

TIME SERIES COMPARISON

Shows changes over time

TIME SERIES COMPARISON
LINE CHARTS

▶ **43**

Chart 43 is a simple line chart that shows changes over time when you have many periods. Two graphic treatments are used: (1) the solid line for the actual is distinguished from the dashed line for the forecast; and (2) the arrows emphasize the direction and amount of change.

Projected growth seems unrealistic in light of recent performance

1977 78   79   80   81   82   83 1984   1989

Charts 44 through 53 are examples of grouped or multiple line charts.

As Chart 44 shows, when lines cross, use different patterns (e.g., dotted, dashed, solid, thick, thin) to eliminate confusion; when lines do not cross, this is not necessary. In any case, the bolder, solid line should be reserved for the most significant item.

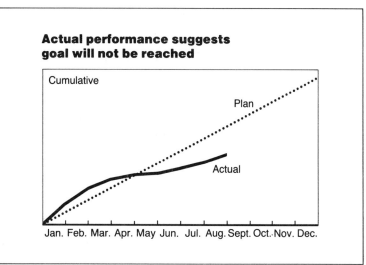

Actual performance suggests goal will not be reached

Cumulative

Plan

Actual

Jan. Feb. Mar. Apr. May Jun. Jul. Aug. Sept. Oct. Nov. Dec.

The wavy line at the base of Chart 45 indicates that the bottom of the vertical scale has been cut. In this case, the focus is not on the relative levels of revenue versus expenditures (in that event, the chart should be plotted from the zero line) but on the differences between the two. Here, different shadings are used to distinguish surplus from deficit.

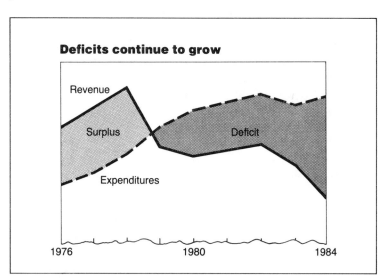

Deficits continue to grow

Revenue

Surplus

Deficit

Expenditures

1976   1980   1984

▶ 46

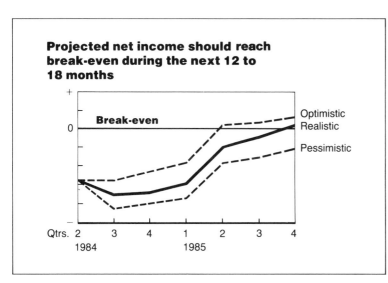

Projected net income should reach break-even during the next 12 to 18 months

Chart 46 provides a cushion of safety when showing projected data. Establishing an optimistic/pessimistic range around the best-guess (realistic) trend line reduces the risk of being held accountable for a projection that is tenuous at best, no matter what the assumptions are. In this case, thin dashed lines are used to establish the range; shading the range would also work.

▶ 47

Home buyers are caught in the crisscross of decreased building and increased construction costs

Units   Costs

Number of units

Construction cost

1974   '76   '78   '80   '82   1984

Chart 47 is a multiple scale chart (i.e., different scales to the left and right) which brings together for close comparison two or more curves that are measured either in different units or are so far apart in size that they would be difficult to compare. If you wish to compare change or growth, make the zero lines of both scales coincide and select the scale intervals so that both curves meet at some meaningful point. Better still, convert both series to a common base (e.g., index numbers or percentage changes) and use only one scale.

Chart 48, plotted against a logarithmic (semilog) scale, shows the rate of change from any point to any other point in a series of data. On this kind of chart, absolute figures increasing at a constant rate (e.g., 5 percent each week) would be shown as a straight line; on an arithmetic scale chart, absolute figures increasing at a constant 5 percent rate would appear as a curving line slanting up at a steeper and steeper angle.

Since there is no zero line, this chart should not be used to measure levels, magnitudes, or negative data. It cannot legitimately be shown as a surface chart (or a column chart). Always use logarithmic scales with caution; if there is any chance that the reader may not understand the scale, explain how to read it and what to look for.

▶ 48

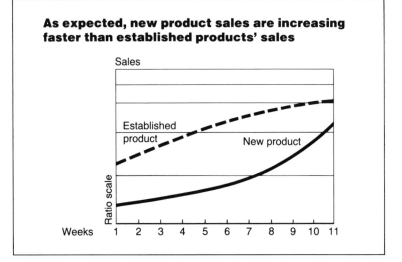

As expected, new product sales are increasing faster than established products' sales

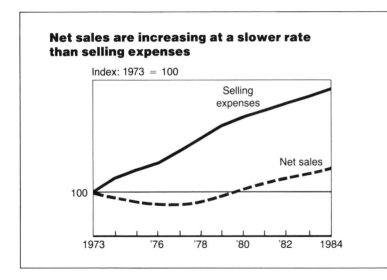

Net sales are increasing at a slower rate than selling expenses

Index: 1973 = 100

Selling expenses

Net sales

100

1973   '76   '78   '80   '82   1984

► **49**

Chart 49 is an index scale chart, which shows data that have been converted into percentages of a base value. Unlike the logarithmic scale chart, which shows the relative change between *any* two points in time, the index scale chart shows the relative change only from the base value for each period. It offers an advantage over absolute amount scales since it can be used for comparing two or more series of data that are measured in different kinds of units or in different-sized units. This kind of comparison may be clearer if changes are presented as simple percentage differences. For example, "Percentage increase in sales since 1973" shows exactly the same picture as "Index of sales: 1973 = 100," except that in the former the scale is divided to read 0, 25 percent, 50 percent, instead of 100, 125, 150.

▶ 50

Instead of index values, Chart 50 uses a scale that shows percentage changes between 1980 and 1984. To provide meaningful comparison between the three items—income, assets, and sales—the scales must be the same for all three. An option here is to show only two charts, one for Company A and one for Company B, and to plot each company's percentage change in income, assets, and sales on its own grid.

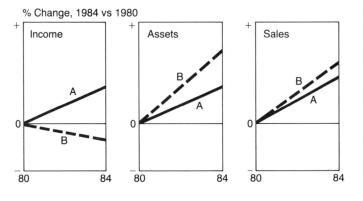

Company A outperformed company B despite B's greater growth in assets and sales

% Change, 1984 vs 1980

▶ 51

Chart 51 uses a calculation tree to visualize a mathematical formula—in this case, return on investment equals return on sales multiplied by investment turnover. In each window, the trend for two companies is shown, allowing the reader to study the various branches of the tree for the source of any problem in the resulting ROI performance.

Company A's ROI remains better than Company B's

▶ 52

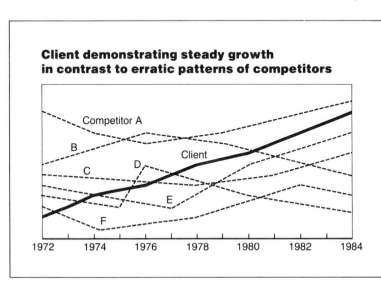

Client demonstrating steady growth in contrast to erratic patterns of competitors

In Chart 52, the line representing the client is emphasized as a bold solid line and is compared to the lines for *all* competitors. If, on the other hand, you want to compare the client to *each* competitor, the technique in the next example is more appropriate.

▶ 53

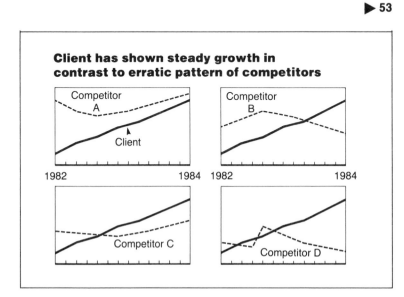

Client has shown steady growth in contrast to erratic pattern of competitors

Chart 53 contains more charts (and therefore requires more drafting time) since it compares the client separately to each competitor, but the comparison per chart is simpler than in the previous example. The client line is identical on each chart. Using this approach, you can group the comparisons for easy reading (e.g., by competitors who were ahead, about the same, or behind the client at a given point in time). You might also emphasize client performance by using a surface chart rather than a curve.

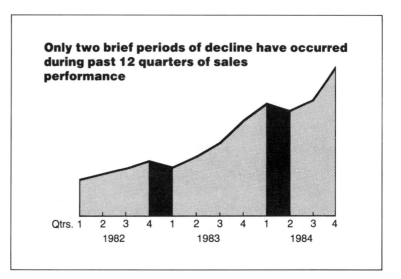

▶ 54

Only two brief periods of decline have occurred during past 12 quarters of sales performance

Qtrs. 1 2 3 4 1 2 3 4 1 2 3 4
        1982   1983   1984

Chart 54 is a surface chart, a line chart with the space between the trend line and the baseline shaded to give a greater feeling for quantity. The graphic treatment in this example—darker shading for the periods of decline—calls attention to the two quarters under scrutiny.

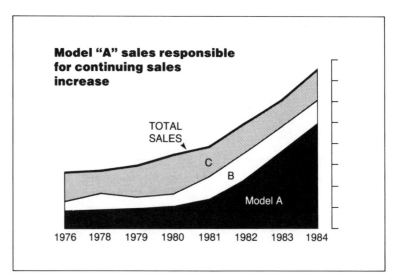

▶ 55

Model "A" sales responsible for continuing sales increase

TOTAL SALES

C

B

Model A

1976 1978 1979 1980 1981 1982 1983 1984

Chart 55 demonstrates the change in the absolute contribution of three components over time, but with the primary emphasis on the total. Only the bottom layer is measured directly from a fixed base. All other layers are measured from a changing base, and their size can be gauged only approximately. To permit direct reading, use the approach illustrated by Chart 39. If the layers fluctuate sharply, use a subdivided column chart (see Chart 38) or the approach illustrated by Chart 39.

▶ 56

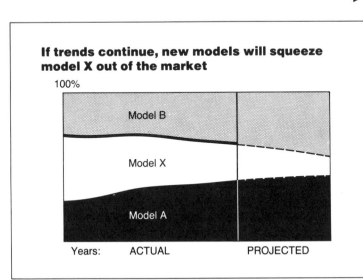

If trends continue, new models will squeeze model X out of the market

100%

Model B

Model X

Model A

Years: ACTUAL   PROJECTED

Chart 56 shows the change in the relative contributions of components over time. The important component—in this case, Model X share—is sandwiched between the two competing models to stress the message. Like all charts illustrating relationships, this type of chart can be misleading if the percentages are based on absolute amounts that are not fairly stable. For example, if 100 percent represents a sharply rising total, a decreasing percentage may actually represent an increasing amount. In such cases, there is a special advantage in picturing the absolute amounts in an accompanying chart or table.

TIME SERIES COMPARISON

Shows changes over time

TIME SERIES COMPARISON
COMBINATION CHARTS

Charts 57 through 63 combine column and line charts to provide additional perspectives on changes over time.

Chart 57 could use grouped columns (that is, one column for capacity and another for orders) but, since capacity is constant, it is shown instead as a background line/surface chart. To emphasize the difference between capacity and orders—instead of their levels, as in this example—an option is to use a deviation chart (see Chart 33) with capacity as the baseline and measuring the number of orders below or above capacity.

▶ 57

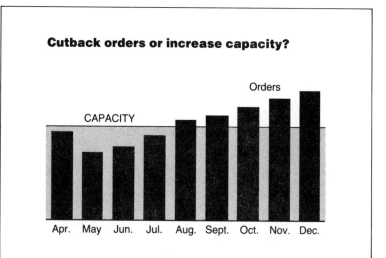

Cutback orders or increase capacity?

▶ 58

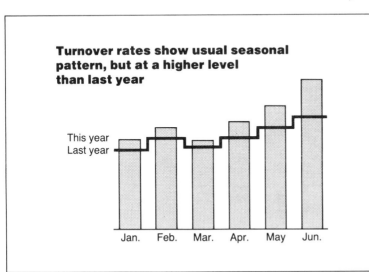

Chart 58, too, could be presented as grouped columns (one column for this year, one for last year). On the other hand, this column and line technique places primary emphasis on the columns representing this year's activity and secondary emphasis on the comparison of this year's versus last year's data.

▶ 59

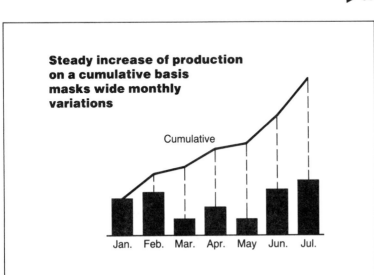

Chart 59 combines a column chart to show the fluctuation in monthly production with a line chart to show the cumulative (sometimes referred to as year-to-date) trend since January.

Chart 60 uses a deviation column chart to show how the initial investments in 1984 and 1985 turn positive in 1986, and a line chart to indicate when the break-even point is achieved.

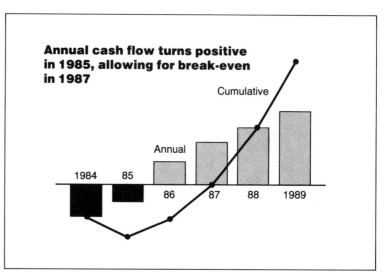

Annual cash flow turns positive in 1985, allowing for break-even in 1987

Cumulative

Annual

1984 85 86 87 88 1989

Chart 61 is similar to Charts 59 and 60 but, in this case, the line represents the net difference between the gains and losses for each month rather than the cumulative trend.

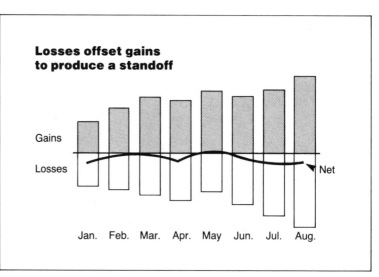

Losses offset gains to produce a standoff

Gains

Losses

Net

Jan. Feb. Mar. Apr. May Jun. Jul. Aug.

▶ 62

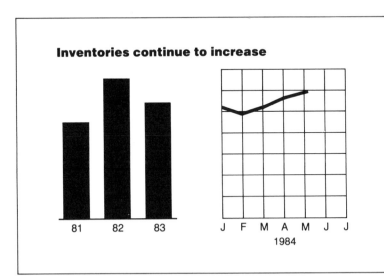

Inventories continue to increase

81 82 83

J F M A M J J
1984

Chart 62 uses columns to summarize past annual data and a line chart to study this year's performance on a month-by-month basis. This technique is often used in management information systems; it leaves space to add monthly performance data, thereby eliminating the need to prepare a new chart each month.

▶ 63

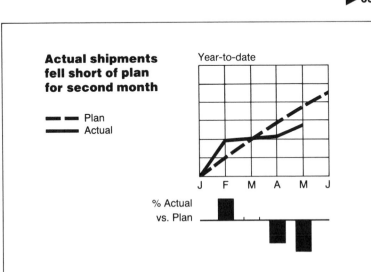

Actual shipments fell short of plan for second month

▬ ▬ Plan
▬▬ Actual

Year-to-date

J F M A M J

% Actual
vs. Plan

Chart 63 is also often seen in company chart rooms. It is a plot of actual monthly (or weekly or quarterly) results against the plan set at the beginning of the year (or against an objective or last year's total). On a cumulative basis, the differences between actual and plan usually tend to be small and often fail to focus attention on problem periods. To magnify these differences, it is a good idea to show the percentage variations of actual versus plan, as illustrated in this example.

Chart 64 combines pie charts with a line chart. The pies show the share mix at each point in time, and the line chart shows the changing totals over time. Keep it simple—not more than three components per pie, not more than one trend line, not more than six periods of time.

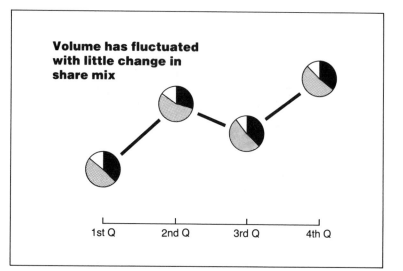

Volume has fluctuated with little change in share mix

1st Q   2nd Q   3rd Q   4th Q

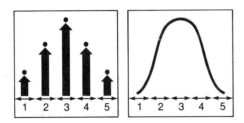

FREQUENCY DISTRIBUTION COMPARISON

Shows how many items fall into a series of progressive numerical ranges

FREQUENCY DISTRIBUTION COMPARISON

▶ 65

Chart 65 shows the histogram form of frequency distribution. Note that the ranges across the horizontal scale are equal and discrete.

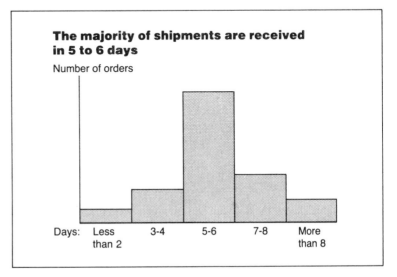

The majority of shipments are received in 5 to 6 days

Number of orders

Days: Less than 2   3-4   5-6   7-8   More than 8

► 66

For continuous data—instead of discrete data as in Chart 65—use the histograph approach shown in Chart 66. Here, the horizontal scale shows the values lined up against the ticks rather than expressed as groups.

Most sales are between $30 and $50

Number of sales

$10   20   30   40   50   60   70   80   90 $100

Size of sales

► 67

Chart 67 combines the step column and step line to compare two distributions in the same chart.

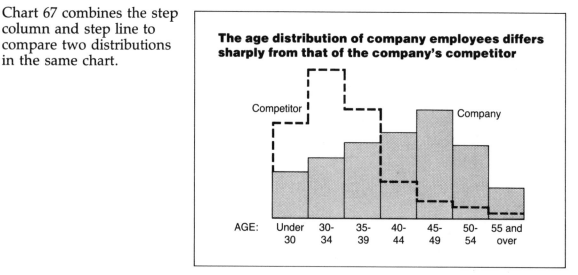

The age distribution of company employees differs sharply from that of the company's competitor

Competitor

Company

AGE: Under 30   30-34   35-39   40-44   45-49   50-54   55 and over

▶ **68**

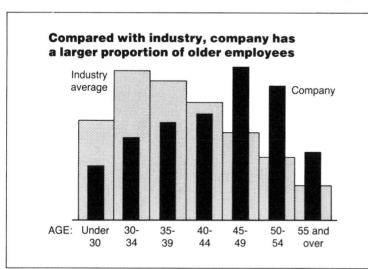

Compared with industry, company has a larger proportion of older employees

Industry average

Company

AGE: Under 30 | 30-34 | 35-39 | 40-44 | 45-49 | 50-54 | 55 and over

Chart 68 combines a column chart for company data and a step-column chart for the industry. This sort of treatment is especially appropriate for this kind of one-against-all comparison. In this case, some of the overlapping columns are bigger than the background columns without creating confusion (see discussion of Charts 19 and 37).

▶ **69**

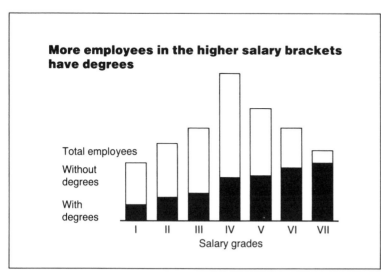

More employees in the higher salary brackets have degrees

Total employees

Without degrees

With degrees

I | II | III | IV | V | VI | VII
Salary grades

Chart 69 is a subdivided histogram that shows, primarily, the distribution of the total number of employees and, secondarily, the components of each salary grade. Here, the salary grade is a shortcut to showing the actual salary ranges.

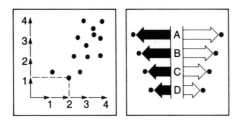

CORRELATION COMPARISON

Shows whether or not the relationship between two variables is as expected

Chart 70 is a dot chart (scatter diagram), which helps determine whether the relationship between two variables follows an expected pattern. In this example, it would be expected that the greater the discount offered, the greater the volume sold. The faint arrow indicates where the expected pattern might fall and highlights the fact that the expected and actual patterns differ widely. Although the dots represent individual transactions, they do not specifically identify the salespersons, since labeling each dot would clutter the chart. An option for identifying specific salespeople is suggested in the following chart.

CORRELATION COMPARISON

▶ 70

There is no relationship between discount and volume sold

There is no relationship between discount and volume sold

Discount   Unit volume sold

C
P
D
B
O
J
M
N
G
H
I
K
A
F
E
L

Chart 71 is a paired bar chart that lets you identify each transaction as well as see the overall correlation. Using the same data as in the previous chart, it ranks the items by size of discount. If the correlation ran as normally expected, the volume bars would mirror the pattern of discounts.

▶ 72

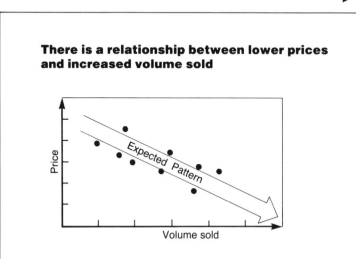

There is a relationship between lower prices and increased volume sold

Price

Expected Pattern

Volume sold

Depending upon the data, the expected pattern could be horizontal (indicating no relationship) or downward, as shown in Chart 72. Here, the dots cluster around the expected pattern pointing out that there *is* a relationship between increasing prices and declining volume sold.

▶ 73

Chart 73 uses the same data used in Chart 72, but presents them as a paired bar chart. In this example, the bars do not form a mirror image, but instead show a consistent pattern between prices and volume sold.

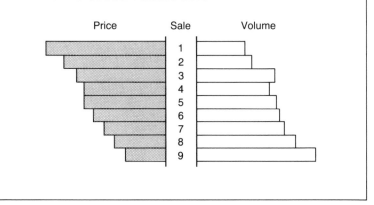

There is a relationship between lower prices and increased volume sold

Price   Sale   Volume

▶ 74

Chart 74 is a grouped dot chart that shows more than one item. To make the distinction between the two items, the chart uses dots and circles; other symbols, such as squares and triangles, can also be used.

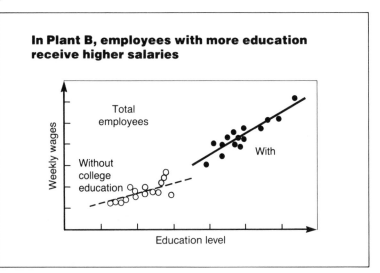

In Plant B, employees with more education receive higher salaries

▶ 75

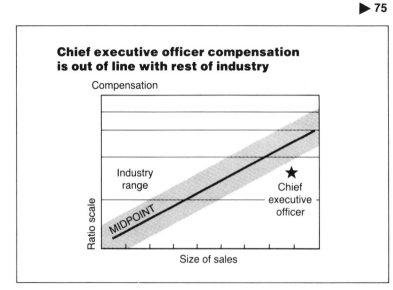

Chief executive officer compensation is out of line with rest of industry

Compensation

Industry range

MIDPOINT

Chief executive officer

Ratio scale

Size of sales

Chart 75 shows a correlation comparison using semilogarithmic scale. The two items in this example are the industry range (perhaps 5 percent above and below the midpoint) and the chief executive officer's compensation relative to his company's sales (shown by the star, the equivalent of a dot). On an arithmetic scale, the industry range would become larger as it moved across the chart, since it is usually computed as a constant percentage increase; it would also curve upward, making it difficult to study the relationships. This scale arrangement clarifies the comparison by "straightening out" the industry relationship and maintaining the range at a visually constant width.

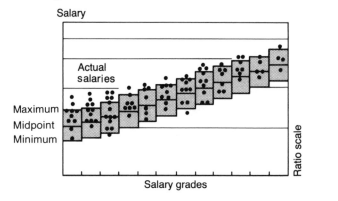

▶ 76

Actual salaries call for reevaluation of salary structure

Chart 76 is similar to Chart 75 except that the range is defined by the maximum, midpoint, and minimum of each salary grade. The dots represent the actual salaries of the employees in each grade and their relation to the range. The reason for reevaluating the structure is that most employees are above the midpoint of their range and many are above the maximum.

▶ 77

Present cost structure provides reasonable profit

Chart 77 is a break-even chart that combines a subdivided surface chart to show costs (fixed and variable) with a line chart to show volume of sales. Although it appears out of place here among the dot charts and paired bar charts, it is used to show the correlation between increasing volume and higher cost. The vertical bar at the right can be added to identify the components of costs at a specific volume of sales.

► 78

Chart 78 has become known as the "bubble chart." It is little more than a dot chart in which dots of differing sizes reflect a third dimension. In this example of a company's business portfolio, each of nine businesses is positioned according to the correlation of market attractiveness and company strength; the farther into the upper right-hand corner, the better the business. The dot representing each business is enlarged into a "bubble" to indicate, in this case, the range of profits contributed by that business.

► 79

Chart 79 takes three of the nine businesses shown on Chart 78 and illustrates each business's movement over time in terms of its profitability measured by the correlation between return on assets and return on spending. Placing each business on its own grid is less confusing than placing all three on one grid. More charts? Yes. But simpler comparisons per chart.

Chart 80. Oops, I'd better quit while I'm ahead.

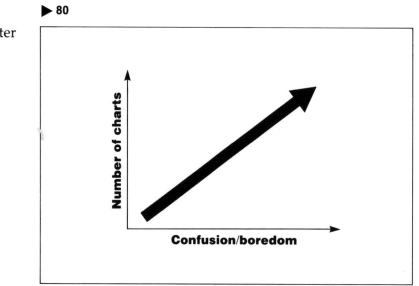

INDEX